THE COMMUNITY
THEATER HAND

THE COMMUNITY THEATER HANDBOOK

A Complete Guide
to Organizing and
Running a
Community Theater

GARY P. COHEN

HEINEMANN
Portsmouth, NH

Heinemann
A division of Reed Elsevier Inc.
361 Hanover Street
Portsmouth, NH 03801–3912
www.heinemanndrama.com

Offices and agents throughout the world

Library of Congress Cataloging-in-Publication Data
Cohen, Gary P. (Gary Philip), 1952–
    The community theater handbook : a complete guide to organizing
and running a community theater / Gary Cohen.
     p. cm.
    ISBN 0-325-00441-2 (alk. paper)
    1. Community theater—Handbooks, manuals, etc. 2. Community
theater—United States—Handbooks, manuals, etc. I. Title.

PN2267 .C64 2003
792′.022—dc21   2002151188

Editor: Lisa A. Barnett
Production coordination: Vicki Kasabian
Production management: Karen Ettinger, TechBooks
Cover design: Jenny Jensen Greenleaf
Typesetter: TechBooks
Manufacturing: Jamie Carter

Printed in the United States of America on acid-free paper
07 06 05 04 03 DA 1 2 3 4 5

I would like to dedicate this book to Michelle Massa,
my friend and theatrical partner,
who pushes me to keep my standards high
when my energy, enthusiasm, and patience are low;
and to my son Zach,
who happily has chosen sports over theater.

Contents

Preface   *xi*

Acknowledgments   *xv*

Overview: What Exactly Is a Community Theater?   *xvii*

1 The Theater Building Itself   **1**

The Proscenium Stage (and Its Respective Curtains)   4

Stage Terminology   9

Variations of the Proscenium Stage   10

Other Areas in the Theater   14

In Summation   17

2 Personnel   **20**

Producer/Board Members/President   21

Creative Staff   24

Various Crews   33

Office Staff   36

Legalities   39

A Presence on the World Wide Web   40

Grants   40

3 Securing the Rights   **42**

Musicals   44

Comedies and Dramas: Straight Plays   *48*

Legal Requirements   *49*

Other Companies   *51*

4   Planning a Season   *53*

Casting the Season   *54*

Precasting   *56*

Technical Considerations   *57*

Getting the Audience into the Theater   *58*

Surveys   *60*

5   Auditions   *61*

Getting the Word Out   *61*

Open and Closed Auditions   *64*

Callbacks   *67*

6   The Rehearsal Process   *72*

Six-Week Rehearsal Breakdown   *72*

Tech Week   *74*

7   Technical Aspects   *81*

Set Design   *81*

Costumes   *91*

Lighting   *95*

Props   *108*

Special Effects   *110*

Scenic Painting   *114*

Sound   *118*

Intercom Systems   *123*

**8   The Director   *125*

Research   *125*

Preproduction Work on the Script   *128*

Working with Actors   *130*

Theater Games and Acting Exercises   *132*

Thoughts on Staging   *133*

**9   Theater Essentials   *138*

Items to Keep on Hand   *138*

Additional Concerns to Address   *140*

The Many Uses for Computers   *142*

Conclusion   *145*
Glossary   *147*
Resources   *153*

Preface

This book might very well have been called *A Life in Community Theater*. For more than thirty years I have been involved, in one way or another, with a community theater. I have stored up enough knowledge, anecdotes, tips, and mishaps to merit this book. At least I hope you'll find it meritorious.

In the early 1970s, while still a Drama and Communications major at Hofstra University on Long Island, I gathered up two of my theatrically inclined friends and suggested to them that we start a community theater. Throughout my teens I had been involved in my high school productions as an actor and had directed and acted at many community theaters in New Jersey.

One of my friends was a dancer and a budding choreographer, and the other was a singer and fledgling musical director, so we seemed to have all the bases covered. Commuting back to my New Jersey home from Long Island on weekends, the three of us set out with naïve enthusiasm to find a home for our new theater, which we would name Celebration Playhouse, after the Jones and Schmidt off-Broadway musical *Celebration*.

Our inquiries took us to a tavern in Roselle Park, NJ, which had an unused banquet room in the basement. Since this venue ultimately didn't pan out, the owner happened to know of a restaurant in the same town that also had a larger but equally underutilized lower-level banquet room. Within a few months, Celebration Playhouse was born.

After but a single season of banquets and parties, as well as diners walking, talking, and often dancing above our heads, we knew that this was not our dream home. We had, however, developed somewhat of a respected reputation, and so when another entrepreneur offered us space in a nearby deserted feed and seed store, as well as the covering of the cost of renovations, we packed our theatrical trunks and moved. Effectively owning our own building, we established a versatile 125-seat black box space (more on black boxes later) and survived for quite a number of seasons before economics and in-house disagreements forced us to sell our rights to theater.

Flashback ten years earlier to 1963: a different group of theatrical enthusiasts approached the Middlesex County Board of Chosen Freeholders, which is a type of government adopted by certain counties in New Jersey (and, I assume, other states), also to start a community theater in a large county-owned park. At that time there was a fairly spacious storage shed in the park, and it was agreed that the troupe could use half of it to perform shows in the summer. Being a line item on the Department of Parks and Recreation's budget, no admission was charged, and this outdoor summer theater grew by leaps and bounds. Eventually, an amphitheater was built on the grounds, and thousands of people attended shows each summer at what is affectionately called Plays-in-the-Park at the Roosevelt Park Amphitheater (later changed to the Stephen J. Capestro Theater in honor of one of the enlightened Freeholders who championed the venture). The whole program was unique—a government-funded summer theater!

When a fire destroyed the original theater building in 1975, an effort from the Freeholders, combined with The Green Acres Commission, created a brand new theater building that today houses state-of-the-art equipment and presents shows to 2,000-plus people a night with a $3.00 admission charge for adults.

There is an interesting connection between these two theaters. When my partners and I sold Celebration Playhouse after six successful seasons, I began my association with Plays-in-the-Park. After directing shows for several seasons, I became the Associate Producer and then the Producing Director, a position I have enjoyed ever since. Plays-in-the-Park is one of the largest community theaters in the country.

Between these two extremes there are hundreds of community theaters of varying sizes. I have personally managed the two bookends—the small and the large—and have worked at a great many in between. I've seen them open and close and have studied the whys and why-nots.

Based on my experience, I offer this book to the novice who is looking to start a theater group, as well as to seasoned producers who might like some insight into how others do things. Regardless of your years "in the business," perhaps you'll enjoy the anecdotes and stories and maybe gather a few pointers to make your theater run more smoothly.

If I talk about equipment that your theater doesn't yet have—computerized lighting equipment, wireless body microphones, and the like—please don't get nervous or frustrated or skip that particular passage. You can be successful without such equipment. But knowledge is power, and knowing what state-of-the-art goodies are available gives you something to strive for. In fact, by the time you finish this book, some of what I tout as "the latest" may already be outdated.

Please read this book with a pencil or a highlighter in hand and circle or dog-ear pages when you come across something that you think you might wish to remember later. There's a lot of information in there—you just may have to dig for it.

So "curtain up!"—let's begin. Oh, by the by, *theater* can be spelled *theater* or *theatre*. For my taste, *theatre* is a tad pretentious, unless you're in Britain; therefore I'm going to use the Americanized *theater*. So sue me.

Acknowledgments

I'd like to thank the following people and organizations for all their support in my writing this book and throughout the years:

Thanks to Jennifer Adamowsky, who created many of the illustrations in this book and who designs the website for Plays-in-the-Park; Roman Klima, Master Electrician at Plays-in-the Park, who helped me accurately describe technical points in this book; Patricia Bornhofen from ETC, for allowing use of photos of their equipment and for helping to clarify tricky lighting issues; Steve Schweer of Norcostco, Kelly Salvadore of Rose Brand, Jim Juniper and Marjorie Stacey of Le Maitre, for allowing use of illustrations from their catalogs for this book.

Plays-in-the Park, New Brunswick, NJ; Stephen J. "Pete" Dalina, Department Chair and Ralph Albanir, Director, Middlesex County Parks Department; David B. Crabiel, Director, and Pete Dalina, Deputy Director, Middlesex County Board of Chosen Free-holders, for keeping Plays-in-the-Park alive for forty years!

Overview
What Exactly Is a Community Theater?

In the most general terms, *community theater* might be defined as a "theatrical producing organization serving a limited area and operating under an amateur licensing agreement."

What does all that mean?

Well, a theatrical producing organization is a group of people who put on plays (that's easy), and a limited area is usually a single town or community (hence, the name sometimes associated with the theater—The Jabip Dramatic Club, The Whoseywhatsis Community Players, etc.).

An amateur licensing agreement means that when the producing organization calls one of the licensing companies that control the amateur rights for the major musicals (see Chapter 3) they pay royalties and rental fees based on an amateur status.

I would think that this criterion alone most defines a community theater, but a theater can also be defined by what it is not—a community theater is not a professional theater, a regional theater, or a college or high school theater.

The organization of a community theater can take many forms, but the traditional ones (some of which have been in existence well over seventy-five years) take the form of a "club." Usually everyone involved is a volunteer. An organization is set up with not-for-profit status, and thus can make tax-free purchases. The governing board (perhaps for a two-year term) might be made up of a president, a few vice-presidents (such as membership, correspondence, etc), a few secretaries, and a treasurer. There might be a board of directors (often six people for a three-year term) who meet monthly in regard to managing all the other committees. Or, in a less structured environment, it might be just a handful of dedicated folks assuming all the positions for as long as they feel like being in charge.

And then there are all the subcommittees, such as Lobby, Program, Grounds, Lighting, Sound, Costumes, Building and

Maintenance, Publicity, Fund Raisers, Play-Reading, Nominating, Ushers, Set Decorating, Set Painting, Box Office, Props, Set Construction, Art Display, Outreach (educational programs coordinated with schools), Hospitality (for parties and dances and other nontheatrical social events), and on and on and on. I've worked in theaters where there is a separate chairperson and numerous volunteers running each of these departments, and I've been with theaters where a few people have done it all.

While some community theaters are housed in the same building for years, there are also established groups that rent the local high school or community center and don't have a permanent home. They often give a portion of the box office take to the venue or pay a set fee up-front.

The actors are volunteers—I've yet to see a community theater that pays its actors—in fact, they may even be asked to pay a fee to become a member of the club before they can appear in a show. While I've experienced shows where one Equity actor is brought in under a Guest Artist Contract, this is most certainly the exception. The more benevolent theaters offer a few free tickets to some performances to offset this membership fee, which I always felt was good for public relations.

The creative staff (director, choreographer, musical director, designers) may or may not receive a small stipend. The crews (props, set painting, follow spot operators, etc.) are usually volunteers.

I've noticed one thing, however—musicians rarely work for free, and so musicals can become very expensive. They are often worth it, both in a creative sense and in a revenue-generating sense, but producers must be very careful. The expense is high, but nothing can ruin a production quicker than amateur musicians that can't cut the score. It is most often worth the expense of paying for professionals, even if you just use a piano, drums, and bass.

While there are no hard and fast rules, the "club" type of community theater tends to produce shows that are very commercial in nature—and shows that can utilize a great number of participants. Generally speaking, the more people involved in the productions, the larger the audiences—at least in terms of relatives and friends of the cast and crew.

Here you'll often find a season of Neil Simon-type comedies, with maybe one or two well-known Jerry Herman or

Rodgers and Hammerstein musicals thrown in. Perennial favorites such as *Joseph and the Amazing Technicolor Dreamcoat* or *Godspell* seem to be the stock-in-trade of a great many community theaters. When dramas are done, they are likely to have somewhat of a household name, such as *The Mousetrap, Inherit the Wind, Twelve Angry Men,* etc.; family entertainment usually is the norm.

Once an established community theater has found its recipe for success, it often varies its menu with shows of a more experimental nature. It all depends upon the board members and their willingness to broaden their, and the audience's, horizons.

Some community theaters are managed more like regional theater, where the owner(s) or founder(s) do not answer to a board but rather make all the decisions themselves. These types of community theaters are less prevalent than the "club" type and can walk a very dangerous line between success and failure. Their seasons are often top-heavy with shows that the owner/founder prefers, and this can lead to a shortage of variety. If the locale of the theater—say, for example, an artsy summer resort town—meshes with the taste of the producer, then a season of off-off-Broadway avant-garde works might be a tremendous success. But to try and force this perspective on a more general audience can lead to failure. Megalomania can be a very quick road to a short career as well when one person tries to take on all the facets of managing a theater. Theater can be a clash of egos—and it is a very precarious "balancing act" that a producer must walk to get all these talents to function cohesively.

I talk from experience. The aforementioned Celebration Playhouse, which I co-founded a long, long time ago in a galaxy far, far away, was one such theater. It lasted only about five years and was brought down for many reasons, but high among them were demanding egos. Still, the theater shone very brightly during its brief run.

There is also a third type of community theater, and it is the rarest of all. This is a theater that is sponsored in whole by a local government body, be it on a township or county level. I know Plays-in-the-Park was one of the first, and more and more theaters of this type are springing up. It reflects an enlightened government, which realizes that the quality of life is heightened when the arts are part of the community.

This book is intended as an overview of all types of community theaters. I will cover the producing aspects in the early chapters and then go into some technical information in the later chapters. With this in mind, there will be something for everyone—the producer, the director, the designers, the crews, the stage managers, and so on. The only people I won't tackle are the actors. We'll leave that to Stanislavsky.

There are myriads of subject-specific books out there if you wish to further develop your skills as a lighting designer or costumer, or if you are interested in the latest state-of-the-art sound equipment. This book will speak in broader, more general terms. But I will certainly stick in my two cents when I am familiar with or especially like a piece of equipment or a manufacturer of a product, and then you can do your own research if you need more information.

We live in an electronic age, and the Internet is a very wonderful place to spend your free time. It is quite valuable in our profession, as it can serve as a wonderful place to promote your theater as well as a most important way to keep up with theatrical technology and research. Most manufacturers have websites— visiting them can keep you up to date. Whereas the basic principles of directing, choreographing, and producing will remain eternal, lighting and sound equipment can be upgraded almost as soon as you buy the piece of hardware, much like computers. It pays to stay up to date, even if only for your own edification. You can research anything on the Internet—from costumes to props to history. As a producer/director, a good part of my day is spent on the computer, looking up one thing or another.

Speaking of websites, you might try searching out the websites of other community theaters to see what others are doing across the country. The theater at which I am Producing Director—Middlesex County's Plays-in-the-Park—has a website that I encourage you to visit. The URL is *www.playsinthepark.com*. We've been around since 1963, and the site has a lot of good information. Plus feel free to email me with any questions concerning your theater (*pipoffice@playsinthepark.com*), and I promise to answer you to the best of my ability.

We'll soon take a look at actual theater spaces, but first there is one last thought that belongs in this introduction.

Before any community theater begins its life, a MISSION STATEMENT should be created. The purpose of the mission statement is to define for anyone involved in the group exactly what the aims, goals, and purposes of this particular theater are. This mission statement might even be revisited every few years to make sure it is on track and to reflect any changes in policies.

The mission statement should also be included in any sort of legal document created among the business partners, board members, landlord, insurance agency, accountants, and the like. But even the most casual groups who might only do one play a year at a rented facility should still define their goals.

At its most elementary level, it might read something like this:

> The Hatstown Community Theater is founded on the principle that affordable, quality theatrical entertainment shall be presented to the Community utilizing local talent of all ages. The shows chosen shall be suitable for the entire family. An outreach program shall be instituted to bring selected portions of our shows to local schools, hospitals, and care centers.

Of course, statements tend to be much more involved than this example, but regardless of its complexity, it is a very useful tool in helping the theater realize its goals and stay on track.

It's a good place to start—especially in the initial planning stages. It can go a long way to making the right decisions in every other area.

The Theater Building Itself

This chapter is about finding the physical space to start your theater. If you already have your space, then you might find information here that will help either to improve the space or to better utilize it.

In my experience in community theater I learned that two things are true where theatrical venues are concerned:

1. Almost any space that can safely hold people can be used to present plays.
2. Some spaces are infinitely better than others.

I have worked on stages that were housed in barns (yes, truly), supply sheds, Churches and Temples (quite common), restaurants and catering halls, tents, gymnasiums, basements, and, believe it or not, even in theaters.

As discussed in the introduction to this book, my first experience in starting a community theater led me to a restaurant that had a catering hall on the main level and another in the basement. We made a deal to use the basement as a theater. We built a small stage, bought some used lighting equipment, secured 100 old movie seats, and figured that if we did the right vehicles—small, off-Broadway types of shows—we might just do well.

Our first show was the delightful, perennial favorite mini-musical *The Fantasticks*. All through the rehearsal period, which was mostly weeknights and Saturday afternoons (quiet times at the restaurant), we were in our naïve glory. Our theater was about the same size as the Sullivan Street Playhouse, where *The Fantasticks* played in Greenwich Village in New York for over forty years, and aside from some noise emanating from the bar above us, all seemed nice and acoustically sound.

Then came our opening night—a Friday—and aside from the fact that there was barely enough parking to satisfy the theater crowd and the participants of the wedding shower booked into the catering hall above us, there was nothing to prepare us for what happened next.

Right as El Gallo stepped forward to sing the lovely ballad "Try To Remember," the electric guitars and piano from the combo kicked in above us, and the "Bunny Hop" began. The ceiling sagged under the jumping partygoers, our lights bounced up and down, and El Gallo was drowned out. Follow . . . follow . . . follow . . . follow.

A tremendous lesson was learned that evening—research the venue thoroughly before taking any further steps. Needless to say, at the first available opportunity we changed venues.

The second home for Celebration Playhouse was a converted storefront that once housed feed and seed. We were nothing if not adventurous in our choice of structures. It worked rather well— but we had to be very selective in the type of show we produced. It was a black box space, which by theatrical definition means four walls, a flexible playing area, and a flexible seating arrangement with no proscenium, wings, or backstage area.

So here are a few criteria to seek out when looking for a place to put on your shows:

The building needs to be structurally sound, obviously, and zoned for commercial use. You also need to find out if it will be approved for the anticipated amount of people you hope to have in attendance. Legally, parking sometimes impacts on that decision. Check with the local fire department, police department, and zoning department.

Royalties are based, in part, on the number of seats you have available to fill, coupled with the admission charge—something to keep in mind if an old 1,400-seat vaudeville house falls into your hands. You might wish to remove or rope off some seats if 1,400 seems a tad ambitious for your first season. You can then base your royalties on 1,000 or 800 seats, for example.

The proper location is a major consideration. People want to feel safe if they leave the theater at 11 P.M. An area offering a few nice restaurants within reasonable distance will help draw people. They can dine before or after and make a night of it.

A local sports bar or restaurant can also become the best friend of your staff and cast, who most always feel the need to unwind somewhere after a show. Strike up an ongoing relationship with the establishment, and the publicity possibilities and reciprocals are endless; plus, it is always nice to feel welcomed by the folks who wait on you and the rest of your staff.

While an isolated barn in the boondocks or an outdoor amphitheater in a park might make for a wonderful summer theater, it is not as conducive for year-round operation. If there is heavy snow, will the audiences be able to get to the theater? A location in an upscale artistic community will have a built-in audience of people already interested in the arts, and the more restaurants, galleries, and interesting stores in the vicinity, the better.

The best buildings have adjacent parking dedicated to the building. It is hard enough to get an audience into a theater these days; you will lose some people if they have to park far away, or struggle to find a spot. It is much worse if they have to pay for parking.

The building needs a high ceiling. While few spaces outside of a legitimate theater have a ceiling so high that the pieces of scenery and curtains can be stored above the stage and "flown" in when required, too low a ceiling and your lighting possibilities will be severely limited. Twenty-foot ceilings are fine; thirty-foot ceilings are great. That's why churches or old movie theaters often make great community theaters. Unfortunately, many improvised black box theaters—housed in odd facilities—have low ceilings, requiring either mini-lighting instruments or major renovations.

You will also need to conform to the rules and regulations of the ADA (Americans with Disabilities Act). Check to see if the building houses properly accessible bathrooms and has ramps and handicapped parking spots—if not, you will most likely have to do some renovations.

You can get information by contacting:

Office on the Americans with Disabilities Act
Civil Rights Division
U.S. Department of Justice
P.O. Box 66118
Washington, DC 20035-6118
202-514-0301
202-514-0383

As far as the stage area is concerned, there are several types. If you are lucky enough to be designing and building from scratch, then any or all of these might be options. But if you are fitting your performance space to an existing configuration, you need to carefully plan what will work best.

The Proscenium Stage (and Its Respective Curtains)

The Broadway standard (and most high school and performing arts centers as well) is the proscenium stage. Usually the stage is three to six feet off the ground and is enclosed by a brick, cement, wood, or curtained proscenium that separates the audience from the stage.

The proscenium opening is generally fairly large and is based on how high the ceiling or fly space is. For example, the

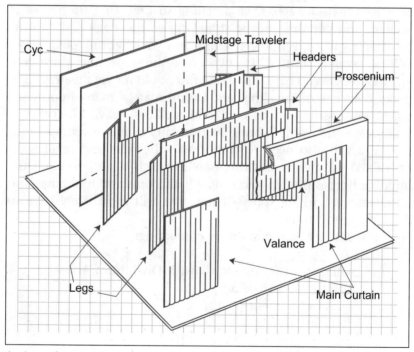

A view of a proscenium stage—main curtain, valance, legs, borders, cyc
Illustration by Kelly Salvadore, from the Rose Brand Catalog

proscenium at Plays-in-the-Park is forty feet wide by sixteen feet high—this is the "window" through which the audience sees the show. The actual ceiling goes up farther, and our battens (pipes) that hold scenery and lighting equipment trim (meaning the position they are kept at during a performance), is about twenty feet, so the battens aren't visible through the proscenium opening.

Most likely, the proscenium opening holds a main curtain, often affectionately referred to as the "main rag." This is made of heavy velour-type material, usually in a gold, red, or blue color, and is either center split—which means half of the curtain travels on from stage right and half travels on from stage left, meeting and slightly overlapping at the center—or the whole curtain flies up and down from a fly loft way above the stage. Really fancy and well-funded theaters might use curtains that "tab" on and off—that means they pull back and up from the center. Other curtains are rigged to be Austrian drapes—pulled up from the bottom by a great many cords, giving a really nice scallop effect. There are also Venetian drapes—which pull up like the Austrian drapes, only the center pulls up first.

There is a valance across the top of the main rag called the main valance. The curtain itself travels on a steel traveler track—which is safely hung from a batten, or pipe. I've noticed some theaters and high schools have the valance on the upstage side of the main rag, and you don't see it when the curtain is drawn closed. I don't favor that configuration myself.

When a curtain is not hung on a traveler track but tied directly to the batten, it is said to be "dead hung."

There are then a series of other valances—called headers or borders—placed every few feet upstage of the proscenium curtain, which is the most downstage piece of soft goods. "Soft goods" is a theatrical term referring to curtains or other scenery made of soft material as opposed to wood, steel, or plastic. These scenic elements are hard goods or hard scenery.

Usually a header is placed just downstage of each electric to further mask both the lighting instruments and the battens themselves.

"What's an electric?," I hear you ask. An electric is a cute name for a pipe or batten dedicated for the purpose of hanging lighting instruments. It usually contains a "raceway," which

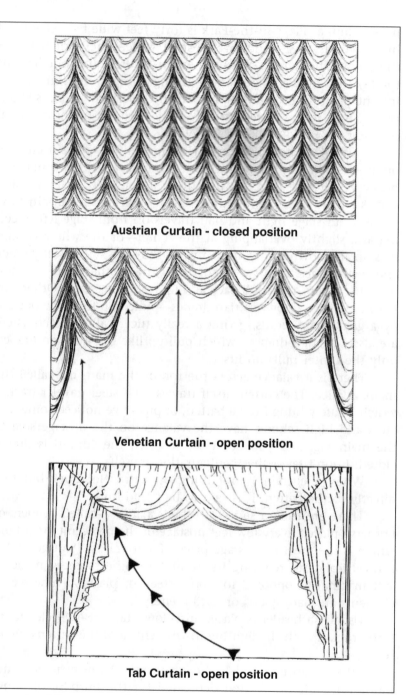

Austrian Curtain - closed position

Venetian Curtain - open position

Tab Curtain - open position

Example of three types of theater curtain styles
Illustration by Jennifer Adamowsky, Related Media

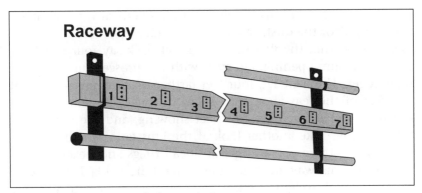

A raceway (connector strips) on a batten
From the Norcostco catalog

is a trough containing cables with electrical outlets every feet or so for plugging in the lighting instruments and numbered so that you can keep track of things. The "plugs" on the end of lighting instruments come in a few varieties—stage pin, twist-lock, three-prong (also known as an Edison plug), and regular two-blade types. You'll want to keep everything in your theater consistent, or you'll wind up having to build a lot of adapters.

Okay, back to the headers, or borders. These are made of various fabrics. Velour is the most expensive and plush, but there are other cotton variations such as duvetyn, Commando Cloth, or Chevron, which are less expensive but still absorb light wonderfully and hang nicely. Check the resource guide at the back of the book for venders who can fabricate the curtains for you and who have catalogs and websites that describe the fabrics in great detail.

Headers run the length of the stage and into the wings a few feet both left and right. Their height is generally three, four, or six feet—whichever is necessary to mask the battens and traveler tracks holding the lighting equipment and other scenery.

At the left and right ends of the headers are legs or teasers. I think the word "teasers" comes from the burlesque days when a stripper might have teased the audience by sticking her leg out from behind it. If it didn't really originate from burlesque, spread the rumor that it did.

The legs are lengths of fabric running vertically, which mask the "wings," or the offstage areas of the stage. Most often they are staggered so that the first set of legs, set back say four feet from the proscenium opening, are even with the proscenium's left and right edges. The next set, four feet farther upstage, are set so that two feet of the legs appear on stage. The next are another four feet back and might have four feet showing, and the last set six feet showing. Take another look at the illustration of the proscenium stage—there you will get an idea of legs and headers.

About halfway upstage there might be a black traveler—which is a lightweight curtain made of black velour or duvetyn, that tracks across the stage from either left or right on a traveler track rigged with a pulley system. During certain types of shows—especially old-fashioned musicals, this black (or any other color) traveler might be brought "onstage," and a scene might be played in front of it while scenery is changed behind it upstage. The midstage traveler might also be of the center-split variety and track on from both the left and the right wings—meeting and overlapping slightly at center stage.

If your theater has fly space—where the battens that hold the scenery and lights can "fly" up and out to double the height of the proscenium—then the use of traveler tracks is not needed. The midstage black traveler will just fly in or out (raise or lower into place) when you need it.

An alternative to the midstage black is to use a painted scenic drop instead. Drops are like travelers only made of unbleached muslin and then painted. You might prefer a painted depiction of a street or a park or a cityscape instead of just a black and would play your scene in front of this while other scenery is changed behind it. Painted drops can fly in and out as well if you have fly space at your theater—which is the best of all possible worlds. It beats pulling a black curtain across the stage any day.

Last, on the upstage-most pipe you might find a "dead hung" cyc. A cyc (short for cyclorama) is a seamless white or light blue fabric that covers the whole visible back of the theater and serves as a backdrop for colored lights, projections of the sky or whatever. It is costly because it is often huge and seamless and should be treated reverently.

Broadway theaters and the like have almost endless resources to fly in all kinds of scenery, both hard (made of wood or steel) and soft (made of fabrics and referred to as soft goods). We should all be so lucky, but occasionally you find college, high school, and community theaters outfitted with some of the aforementioned.

Last, a word about scrims.

The scrim is one of the great theatrical inventions of all time. It is a type of fabric in the gauze family—either the popular "Sharkstooth," or "Bobbinette," which has a more open weave. Scrims can be an effective black masking curtain and also come in white or blue; they can also be painted. Here's the really neat part—when a scrim is lit from the front it becomes opaque—you cannot see through it. But when it is lit from behind, it becomes transparent and you can see the scenery and actors through it.

An example of an effective use of a scrim to create a wonderfully theatrical moment might be to paint a scrim as the exterior of a mansion. Some actors "arrive" for the party in front of the scrim, which is lit just from the front (perhaps we hear the guests inside). And then, we dim the exterior lights and bring up the lights inside, revealing the party in progress. Couple that with the effect of seeing the scrim fly out, and you have magic time.

Stage Terminology

I realize this is a chapter about types of stages, but it might be appropriate for some basic stage definitions to be explained here so that I can freely use this language throughout this chapter and the rest of the book.

All areas on a stage are defined from the actor's perspective—meaning, the actor is standing in the center of the stage looking at the audience. Stage left is the actor's left; stage right is the actor's right. Downstage is towards the audience; upstage is away from the audience. I suppose this method was decided upon because directors are inherently smarter than actors and can quickly recalculate when directing which way to tell the poor actor to enter and exit.

Just a little directorial joke.

The reason for the downstage/upstage decision is that in olden days (we're talking Greek and Shakespearean theater here, not the years prior to *Cats*) most of the stages were "raked"—meaning they were higher upstage and slanted down towards the audience. Therefore, the actor truly walked downhill when he went downstage and uphill when he went upstage.

The stage can be further defined by playing areas—there are usually fifteen of them as shown in the following chart:

UR—up right

R—right

DR—down right

URC—up right center

RC—right center

DRC—down right center

UC—up center

C—center

DC—down center

ULC—up left center

LC—left center

DLC—down left center

UL—up left

L—left

DL—down left

			UPSTAGE BACKDROP			
R3	UR	URC	UC	ULC	UL	L3
					LEG	
R2	R	RC	C	LC	L	L2
					LEG	
R1	DR	DRC	DC	DLC	DL	L1
			DOWNSTAGE			

Okay, onward to different types of theatrical stages!

Variations of the Proscenium Stage

The Apron

A nice addition to the standard proscenium is an "apron" added on downstage of the proscenium. This is not the kitchen variety of apron, of course, but an extension that "breaks" the proscenium wall and allows the actors to step way downstage, bringing them closer to the audience. Often the apron is curved, which has its good and bad points. It looks prettier, but a line of actors on the edge taking a bow or performing certain choreography might very well have to curve as well. Depending upon the placement of the first couple rows of seats, this may be awkward.

Some theaters—particularly old vaudeville houses—might have an orchestra pit in front of the proscenium with a removable covering. The covering is removed during musicals. When the covering is in place, it serves as an apron. A further refinement would be a pit that is actually located under the apron, with the conductor standing in an opening at the most downstage point—this allows for the orchestra to be hidden and for the use of the apron even during a musical when an orchestra is needed.

The apron usually is kept free of scenic elements—except perhaps if the deck itself is painted to resemble cobblestones or such—because when the main curtain is down, the apron is, of course, still visible. But once the play begins, scenic elements and properties are often brought down on to the apron.

Numbers are often placed or painted on the lip of the apron—especially for musicals—so that actors and dancers can judge their placement on the stage. The number "0" would be placed on the centerline, and then numbers would be placed every two feet, radiating from center—such as in the following:

10	8	6	4	2	0	2	4	6	8	10

(I remember loving the Roman Numerals that replaced the usual numbers for the recent revival of *A Funny Thing Happened on the Way to the Forum* with Nathan Lane.)

In the event that an apron is nonexistent, the use of numbers can still be employed by placing them across the lip of the stage at the proscenium line.

Burlesque houses made famous a dramatic variation on the apron called a "passeralle"—or runway—and this still is used, especially in theatrical musicals such as *Gypsy* and *Hello, Dolly!*

A passeralle is a runway that starts at the proscenium line or apron at one end of the stage and wraps around the orchestra, ending at the other end. While this has little use in a dramatic straight play, it does provide for some fun musical numbers. I have used it to great advantage in *The Music Man, Pirates of Penzance* and *Forty-Second Street.* Just be careful in lighting a passeralle, as it presents certain challenges. The position of the audience and the angles of the lighting instruments must be carefully taken into consideration.

Thrust Stages

When the apron extends way into the audience, so much so that people sit on three sides of it, it is called a three-quarter thrust stage. It may still have a proscenium way upstage, but most of the action takes place all along the extended stage. The original Circle in the Square Theater in New York City was a prime example of this type of theater, and a show like *Hot L Baltimore* used this stage to great advantage.

While a three-quarter thrust stage might make for compelling theater in terms of involving the audience—since they sit so close to the stage—it presents quite a number of technical problems. There is the issue of getting set pieces on and off, since there are no curtains to mask things. Oftentimes the actors wind up bringing chairs and tables on along with their entrances. Lighting can be a nightmare, since you have to light the performers from three sides, thus running the risk of lights shining into the eyes of the audience sitting along one of the lengths of the stage.

When these challenges are met brilliantly, a show on a thrust stage can be an exhilarating experience. In the hands of the less talented, it can be annoying.

I have found that three-quarter thrust stages are found primarily in either college or very avant-garde theaters and are not so prevalent today.

Theater-in-the-Round

"Theater-in-the-round" is where the acting area is set up in the center of the theater and the audience sits on all four sides. Entrances are difficult in this type of theater, with actors having to come through the lobby or even exterior doors and fire exits. The problems of sets and lighting are multiplied by this setup; plus there is nothing more disconcerting for an audience member than seeing someone across the stage snoring. It happens.

Only a handful of shows work in the round, but it is certainly cost effective since you simply can't have much scenery. Some purists and experimentalists believe that leaving things to the audience's imagination is always something to strive for in the theater—keeps them thinking. In the round, you simply do not have sets with walls; scenic elements are reduced to furniture for interiors and benches or tree stubs or similar suggestive pieces for exteriors.

Blocking your actors is difficult in the round as you have your back to someone at all times. It takes a perceptive and inventive director indeed to keep the action flowing enough so that the audience is not bothered by clumsy blocking and not made nauseous by too much activity. I have seen everything from Chekhov to Neil Simon in the round, and it's a hit-and-miss affair at best.

Musicals are even harder to stage in the round. Many years ago, where I live in New Jersey, there was a music tent where they would mount large musicals in the round, often with famous stars. You would go really to see the stars, not to see the show mounted as it was originally meant to be staged. While it was a rare treat to watch Zero Mostel cavort in *A Funny Thing . . .* so close to the audience, the musical itself barely resembled the original—gone were the three wonderful multileveled Roman houses that played such an important part in the Broadway staging.

The Black Box

A very common theater configuration is what is referred to as a "black box." This is quite common among community theaters since many are housed in such odd and diverse venues.

A black box is merely an empty space with a portable stage and portable seating, opening up endless possibilities.

Theatre-in-the-round is certainly a possibility in a black box space, but it comes with all the inherent problems. A three-quarter setup, however, works very well in a black box situation. By keeping the audience on only three sides you allow for a back wall to support some sort of scenic element. A friend of mine recently directed a production of *Vanities* in such a space, using the back wall to hang many different sizes and shapes of mirrors, reflecting the title's dual meaning. Another friend directed *Pride and Prejudice* at another theater with a similar setup. I designed the set, and down on the thrust were furniture, rugs, etc., but against the back wall were actual architectural pieces—walls with crown and chair molding as well as framed paintings and draperies, as well as the archways from other rooms and glass doors from the garden. Curtains were hung to act as a sort of false proscenium, allowing for upstage entrances and exits from the backstage area.

If you are the artistic director or producer of a black box theater space, one fun thing is to change the configuration with each play during your season. This keeps the audience interested and the actors, designers, and directors from getting stale.

When trying to utilize a black box theater in terms of lighting, the smartest thing to do would be to have your electrician install a criss-cross grid of pipe on the ceiling. Lighting is so difficult in a black box—you need every option available to you—and a grid of squares would allow for this. This is similar to the way television studios—where they frequently have to change their set configurations—conquer the lighting challenge. This gives you endless lighting positions. Your designer must not only light the actors well but also keep the lights from blinding the audience.

If you are using folding chairs or even theater seats that are all on ground level, you should consider raising the stage by using a platform. This needs be nothing more than four-foot by eight-foot pieces of three-quarter-inch plywood raised up on legs.

It would be better to use stadium seating for the audience—elevating them instead of the stage. You might go three or four rows deep; each row raised up eight inches from the one in front. Stagger each row so that the seats in alternate rows fall between two seats in the rows in both front and back. This will allow everyone to see. You can also put a row of seats on floor level if you need additional seating at any given performance.

Other Areas in the Theater

You must consider the layout of areas other than the stage and seating areas. You will need at least two dressing rooms (unless you believe in unisex dressing rooms—sort of an Ally McBeal thing) with access to the stage from the back of whatever type of configuration you have. I've been in theaters where the access is through the audience, and while it can be done, it is not ideal. Of course, in the case of theater-in-the-round, some entrances and exits would have to be through the audience. And in a thrust situation, you might use a combination—some entrances made from the backstage area and others from the lobby.

What follows is a list of other possible areas, or departments, that might be a part of your theater, based on space, budget, and resources.

Scene Shop

Few are lucky enough to have this, and many have to rent space elsewhere or hire outside production companies to build scenery, but if possible, a space dedicated to building scenery is a wonderful asset. Ideally it would be outfitted with a table saw, a radial arm saw, a drill press, a lathe and other power tools, as well as a full array of hand tools. There would be room to stock lumber and scenic hardware such as turnbuckles, shackles, nicropress fittings, wire rope thimbles, angle braces, and all the other necessities of a scene shop. The actual building of the sets is best left to carpenters and technical directors, so if you aren't familiar with the language of the scene shop don't fret. Suffice it to say a dedicated scene shop is a wonderful thing indeed.

Costume Shop

To the costume designer and stitchers, a room of their own is a major blessing. Complete with sewing machines, surgers, racks, cutting table, storage, and all the tools of the trade, the costume shop is a very important facility, even if you rent all your costumes (there are always alterations to be done!).

Prop Shop

A prop shop or prop area should include tables to work on, lots of hand tools, lots of craft supplies, and lots of storage.

Electrics Area

For whatever reason, anything to do with lighting, special effects and even sound falls under the category of "electrics." You'll note that, as noted earlier, "electrics" also refers to the actual batten that holds the electrical raceway and lighting equipment. It's a versatile word, and although I'm not sure if this is a real word or not, you'll use it if you are in theater. As long as we are discussing vocabulary, note: bulbs in theater are called lamps, so don't tell the master electrician you are going to change a bulb. Lighting fixtures are called instruments. To really confuse things, there are PARS that are lighting instruments and PARS that are lamps, but more on this in the lighting chapter. An electrics room would be a place to store all the expensive lighting equipment and peripherals, to work on repairs, and to inventory what we call "disposables"—items such as gels and gobos which eventually burn out.

Scenics Area

The painters of your sets and scenery are called scenics. They would also love to have an area to call their own. What they need most is a huge slop sink and, after that, shelves for paint, tables to work on, and lots of brushes, rollers, dye, and of course, paint.

Production Office

With a desk or two, a filing cabinet, a computer, and bookshelves, a production office is a necessary space to get business done— whether it is phone work or paperwork, research or meetings; it is even a place to escape.

Ticket Booth and/or Lobby

You need to sell tickets. More and more this is being done via the Internet, and phone sales are also a good method for taking orders, but there will always be a portion of the theater-going public who want to come to a box office, check out the seating chart, avoid paying a service charge, and choose their own tickets.

A ticket booth can be as simple as a table and a cash register or as complex as dedicated rooms behind Plexiglas, outfitted with a computer and ticketing software. Just be aware that to operate this necessity you need a human being working the computer/register—one whom you can trust and is personable—and this could be an expense to the theater. My father always said expense is the enemy of profit, so budget accordingly.

You will need posted and strictly adhered to hours of operation. Nothing will turn off a customer faster than to drive to the box office, expecting it to be open and finding it closed. (When I ran Celebration Playhouse my mother used to work the box office for us—she was very proud of her "son the theater owner"—but you can't always count on family members, so think the box office situation through carefully.)

People often arrive at the theater early, and even if you open the doors to the theater a half-hour before curtain, you need to put the early birds somewhere. A well-heated lobby is always appreciated and will also give you a position from which to sell refreshments and souvenirs. There is a lot of extra revenue to be made in the sale of T-shirts, buttons, key chains, souvenir playbills, and similar merchandise. If you buy in bulk at the local discount outlet (such as a Costco or BJ's wholesaler), you can sell soft drinks and candy and make some nice revenue as well.

One last item: put a boom box in each of these areas. Creative people like to have music playing, especially show tunes.

In Summation

"Theater" can really be produced virtually anywhere and in any space—it depends on your expectations and those of your audience. Between the grand old proscenium-style theater with its luxurious fly loft and wing space, rococo interior, overhanging balcony, and gorgeous chandeliers—and the converted retail store with a communal dressing room in the basement and 125 folding chairs—lies every imaginable configuration. I've seen both extremes work and both extremes fail, because regardless of the space, it's the actors, creative staff, and material that make the difference.

I think it all goes back to that old mission statement. Your venue should reflect and support the type of theater you intend to offer.

If your goal is to re-create Broadway musicals on as close a scale as possible to the original, then you would need to replicate a Broadway house as closely as possible. This would mean a proscenium house with an opening of at least forty feet by thirty feet, with a large apron. You'd need an orchestra pit that can house at least twenty-six musicians comfortably. Seek plenty of wing space left and right for storing scenery and a fly loft with loads of winched (or better yet—electric battens) for flying scenery and lighting instruments. You would benefit from tracks in the stage deck for rolling scenery wagons on and off. Count on hundreds of lights—most with color scrollers and several "intelligent" lighting instruments such as High End Studio Spots, all controlled by hundreds of dimmers and a top-of-the-line computer board. You'd also want enough body microphones to amplify all the principals and most of the supporting cast and quite a few area microphones to pick up the ensemble. How about at least 1,500 seats? And a huge budget.

But if your goal is to rethink musicals to present on a smaller scale or do classic modern comedies and dramas (*Deathtrap, Brighton Beach Memoirs, Noises Off, Lend Me A Tenor, That Championship Season,* to name but a few) then you can scale back the theater as well.

In fact, the great majority of community theaters operate on this smaller scale—precious few have Broadway-style facilities.

The following scenario is within the grasp of many community theaters:

It is not uncommon to have a proscenium house with a thirty-five-foot by twenty-foot opening. Maybe there is no fly area, but the ceiling is often high enough for battens that hold travelers, allowing your soft goods to track on left and right from the wings. Maybe this wing space is modest, but generous enough to store clever scenery—scenery that can fold up and that might even be able to double into different scenes. By painting "flats" on both the front and the back, you can sometimes get two scenes out of the same piece of scenery and still create the illusion of lush sets.

Take the hat shop in *Hello, Dolly!*, for example. The exterior of the shop is painted on a series of flats that roll on via castered platforms. When the characters enter the shop, the flats revolve to reveal the interior painted on the opposite side. One of the flats might even have a door built into it, allowing the characters to step through it as the flats revolve. Stagehands, dressed in black—or even in costumes!—can do the movement or, as I often like to do, utilize the ensemble to move scenery in some creatively theatrical way. This sure saves on volunteer stagehands and gives the ensemble more stage time. (By the way, scenery moved in front of the audience is said to be done "au vista.")

Many community theaters are able to have a nice dressing area for women and another for men, and as long as you stock up on Febreze and keep the windows open a crack, a cramped space is not too intolerable. It is not unheard of for a small theater to house a tiny production office and a basement that can serve as a prop, carpentry, and scenic shop.

Certainly you might have an area of the lobby where you have constructed a ticket booth, and it opens two hours before each performance and is manned by volunteers.

There is also a small area to sell refreshments (you have a fridge and a microwave).

For lighting needs, you have a good number of fresnels, lekos, and Par Cans (lighting fixtures all—more on these critters later) and a computerized lighting board, and you have a few body and floor microphones with a basic sound mixer. Or maybe you found a used two-scene preset manual board cheap on Ebay and are going to do without microphones—no matter.

Given this scenario—and a lot of ingenuity among the creative staff and backstage crew—many a community theater has thrived for decades, turning out excellent and stimulating work.

So the bottom line is to define your goals and then set out to create a theater that will allow you to realize them.

One last thought—charge appropriate admission. A theater utilizing a full Union orchestra and huge casts would appear to be entitled to charge more than the black box space doing a three-character drama or small-scale musical. This is because the public tends to "perceive" how much they are willing to pay based on their impressions. You want the audience to feel that they are paying a price commensurate with the productions you do—although I realize you can't put a price on talent. I'm assuming you will always strive to utilize the best talent available—no one can ask for more than that.

Personnel

While the specifics of how a theater is managed will vary from venue to venue, certain basic similarities are always present. There is a hierarchy that will usually look something like this:

Board members and/or producer(s) and/or president
    and/or
Artistic director and/or managing director
Creative staff
    Director
    Choreographer (if applicable)
    Musical director (if applicable)
    Set designer
    Lighting designer
    Costume designer
    Stage manager
    Technical director
    Sound designer
Crews
    Carpenters (helmed by the master carpenter)
    Scenic artists (helmed by the charge scenic)
    Stitchers/drapers/cutters (helmed by the costume shop head)
    Electricians (helmed by the master electrician)
    Property artisans (propsters)
    Stage crew (helmed by the crew chief)
    Follow spot operators
    Board operator
Front of house
    House manager
    Box office staff

Ticket takers
Ushers
Lobby workers
Refreshment sellers
Custodial staff/maintenance
Office staff
Publicist
Program creators
Billing department
Person to maintain website
Person to secure grants
Someone in charge of building and grounds

Not every community theater will utilize all of these positions. Several of them might even be combined. Certainly not all of the positions will be paid; the majority will be volunteers.

Let's take a look at them in more detail, shall we?

Producer/Board Members/President

In a professional situation, the producer (or producing organization) would raise the money (or put in their own) and then oversee all the other positions. The producer's job description differs slightly in a community theater. Money is not usually raised for one specific production. While grants are often sought, and a producer should have some expertise in how to write them (there are classes and books available), generally the money comes from box office receipts, merchandising, and even some wealthy benefactors, so raising the money isn't the problem. Managing it, however, most definitely is.

At the very, very tippy top of the community theater pyramid sit the board members or, in some cases, the founder(s). They usually select a producer who is in charge of the daily operation, while they meet monthly or more to check on things. Or perhaps the owner of the theater secures an artistic director to run things. It's a gray area. But maybe if I describe how things are run at the theater where I work it'll shed some light on this vague position.

The producer/president is the most difficult to categorize on a community theater level—but it'll get easier from here—the other positions are more easily defined.

I am a producing director at my theater. That's just my particular title—same job, different name. There is always someone to answer to, and in the case of Plays-in-the-Park, my board of directors is actually the Middlesex County Department of Parks and Recreation, who in turn are governed by the Middlesex County Board of Chosen Freeholders.

Or in the case of a neighboring theater that is housed in a museum, the museum's board is the highest rung, and they hire a producer/artistic director/producing director—call him/her what you will—to run things.

What's in a name? Nothing, I guess. I've worked at theaters where a production manager, either on a show-by-show basis or for a season, handles the job that I would associate with that of a producer. In other theaters, the production manager is the liaison between the heads of the tech departments and the producer/artistic director/president. It gets confusing—but as long as you know your job description, I suppose what you call it matters not.

So what do I do every day? Here's a list, in no particular order.

Preseason

Choose the season's shows (this must pass approval by the "board")

Secure the design and artistic staff

Secure royalties/rights

Order scripts, orchestrations

Prepare and order the season's stock of lumber, hardware, scenic paint, lamps and electrical supplies, costume shop supplies, prop supplies, etc.

Prepare and order capital purchases (major soft goods such as curtains and drops, lighting instruments, major tools for the shop, etc.)

Organize auditions

Prepare and send out press releases

Maintain the website

Oversee set designs, costume designs, lighting designs, and tend to any special needs (*Tommy* and *Evita* need slide projectors, *Guys and Dolls* needs neon, *My Fair Lady* needs a revolving stage—things like this)

Work out "deals" with local vendors (tuxedo rental houses, art supply stores, hardware stores) for bargains, discounts, reciprocals (goods in exchange for an ad in the program, for example).

During the season

Hold weekly production meetings with all creative staff, designers, and crews.

Keep detailed records of expenditures and make sure bills are paid.

Oversee the daily operation of the costume shop, paint department, electrics and sound department, and carpentry shop.

Oversee the box office.

Attend all performances to make sure it all goes smoothly.

I often put in twelve- to sixteen-hour days during the production season—working the staffs during the day and working the shows at night. But there is one minor perk: I make the precurtain speech before each performance, welcoming the audience, which has made me a celebrity at the local A&P!

I mention my work schedule not to be commended for it, but because I want to make the point that running a theater is a very time-consuming job, and if you are doing it while holding down a "real" job, plan for not having much of a life outside the theater.

I have also listed all the duties of a producer/president/artistic director to emphasize that this job is certainly not for everyone. It's an incredible amount of work that demands a mind capable of storing a great many details. Plus there are always the personality issues to contend with when you are dealing with so many creative people—it helps to have a less than volatile personality. Perhaps this is why some theaters have a different "producer" for each show, while others divide the job up among a few people.

At the risk of redundancy, in community theater there is no clear-cut job description for "The Producer/Artistic Director/Board of Directors/Producing Director"—he/she/them simply must do whatever it takes to make sure the show goes on.

Let's go on to some of the other positions in more detail.

Creative Staff

Director

The director is in charge of everything creative that happens on the stage. He or she answers to the producer (or whatever name you use), but everyone else answers to him or her. There are as many women directors as men, but for convenience sake, let me just use the male gender from here on in. He must have the vision of how the show is going to be mounted—whether it is going to replicate as close as possible the original or whether it will be re-interpreted. Among his many jobs, the director meets with the designers to make sure there is a cohesive vision of sets, costumes, lighting, and props. He casts the show along with the choreographer and musical director if it is a musical. Casting might also include input from the producer or board and sometimes even from a casting committee, depending on the theater.

He runs the rehearsals, "blocks" the show (a term that means telling the actors where to go, sit, stand, and what business to do) and coaches the actors in their performances. He organizes the "tech" rehearsals—or "technicals" if you've seen *Noises Off*—during which all the technical elements are set. Light cues and levels are determined and timed, sound effects are created and rehearsed, moving the set pieces on and off are coordinated, costumes are worn and evaluated, props are utilized—all leading up to the final dress rehearsal. Then, depending on agreements made with the theater, the director's job is either finished or the director might stay on to observe performances and give touch-up notes. If the director is finished, this job falls to the ever-trusty stage manager.

Note: casting is tricky, and I have worked at theaters where the producers have final approval. There are also theaters where producers don't even attend the auditions, and you know by now that by producer I am referring to the head(s) of the theater. I have even worked at theaters where casting is done by "committee." I'm somewhat opinionated on the subject. I question the integrity of a producer who doesn't bother to attend auditions—if nothing else he should show his support and establish his position. I am also against the casting committee—there is just no way that six or eight panelists with different backgrounds and varied self-interests can understand the director's needs enough to be of any real value. Picking Miss America by jury, maybe—but casting a show, no. I'm in favor of the producer who attends the auditions and offers the directors constructive opinions, perhaps based on past experience with the performer, perhaps based on an alternative point of view—but who then allows the director to make the final choice himself. In the case of a theater where three or four shows are cast at once, a producer will have to look at the "big picture" and offer input to the various directors for the good of the entire season. If two directors are both vying for the same performer, sometimes the producer will have to intervene and make a final decision based on what they perceive is the bigger of the two roles. Perhaps they can help and suggest an alternate for one of the roles because they have been attending all of the auditions. Be wary of casting committees, I always say!

Choreographer

In a musical, the choreographer is not only applicable but also essential. Even if the show has minimal dancing (*I Do! I Do!* as opposed to *A Chorus Line; Sweeney Todd* as opposed to *Anything Goes; Into the Woods* as opposed to *Sweet Charity*) a choreographer worth his or her salt is invaluable in making the whole show flow as a musical should. When I am directing a musical, I, and my choreographic partner for years, approach the show in this manner: I'll take the numbers where a soloist pretty much just delivers the song ("Little Lamb" and "Small World" from *Gypsy*), and Michelle (that's her name) takes all the numbers where there is dancing or lots of movement. She even uses a rating system to help her plan her workload. "A" numbers are truly dance numbers (sticking with *Gypsy*—"All I Really Need Is the Girl," "Dainty June & Her Farmboys"), "B" numbers are ones with half movement and half dance ("If Momma Were Married" and

"You Gotta Have a Gimmick"), and "C" numbers are those that require clever staging rather than dance steps ("Mr. Goldstone," "Rose's Turn"). This is very helpful in determining the amount of time needed to stage, rehearse, clean, and perfect each number during the rehearsal period, and if this rating system is applied prior to auditions, you can determine the level of dancers you are seeking. Then, with the numbers categorized and divided between us, I will help her with integrating the numbers seamlessly into the staging, and she will help polish the numbers I stage, making said numbers more "musical," for lack of a better word. She's a stickler for precision—and it's amazing the difference that polishing even the most static a number can make.

A choreographer in community theater often finds themselves with a dearth of male dancers. Usually there are females who know their way around the dance floor because of their attendance in local dancing schools, but men are another story. Making them look good is a major challenge confronting a choreographer. Still, there is nothing more satisfying than seeing "The Crap Shooters Ballet" from *Guys and Dolls* performed well by a cast who only five weeks earlier had trouble walking and chewing gum.

The key to good choreography is creating the right dances for the level of your performers and making them look good performing it. If jazz squares and swaying is all they can handle, then as long as they look synchronized and polished and "clean," the audience will love it. Challenge them when you can, but never have them do something that ultimately they won't look good doing. Having a wonderful vocabulary of combinations and steps (which you get through researching everything from old movie musicals to MTV) and having the skill, talent, and eye to apply that language is essential. By language I don't mean dance terms such as *pas de bouree* or *grande jete*—although using dance terms with dancers is a good shortcut to teaching a number—but by language I refer to a combination of steps and moves that can be pulled from your memory book and utilized when needed.

The choreographer is also intrinsic to the audition process for a musical—coming up with dance combinations of varying difficulty for the ensemble, the supporting cast, and the principals.

Musical Director

The "MD," as the musical director is affectionately known, is another musical theater necessity. In community theater, the MD often wears a number of hats. He (or she) might at once be the vocal coach, the rehearsal pianist, the pit pianist and the conductor of the orchestra. Sometimes the MD might be what is called a "playing conductor"—playing the keyboards while conducting the rest of the musicians. He might even be the "Orchestra Contractor"—the person who secures the musicians that play in the pit.

Simply put, in community theater the musical director handles everything musical, and one that is proficient at playing the piano is worth his weight in gold. The musical director is present during casting, making sure the performers can cut the material and that there is a good mixture among the ensemble. He then teaches the vocal music to the cast at early rehearsals, accompanies the dancers and vocalists during rehearsals (or prepares a rehearsal tape which is a sad but often necessary alternative), rehearses the orchestra (whether sixteen pieces or just piano, drums, and bass), and then moves on to conduct and/or play for the performances. If you can find an MD who is adept at all the chores outlined here, do whatever it takes to keep them at your theater!

Set Designer

The typical routine of a set designer is: after getting a copy of the script and sitting down with the director for any special visions they might have, the set designer goes to his or her studio (or basement) and begins the preliminary designs.

The designer starts by analyzing and organizing the scene breakdowns to determine just how many sets will be needed and how they will function. He then decides what parts of the scenery will be "hard"—made of wood or steel—and what will be "soft," such as curtains or painted drops.

He will then do some sketches and go back to the director, for artistic approval, and to the producer, who will look at the ideas in terms of budget. Assuming the director and producer approve, the designer then begins a two-step process.

He will make a model of the set(s) in either half-inch or quarter-inch scale—half-inch scale is preferable to quarter-inch scale which is just too small, and he will do a set of drawings and elevations.

The model is invaluable for all concerned. It actually shows the set in such a way that everyone can grasp what it will look like—in three dimensions. Some directors and others on the artistic staff can't really get a full idea of the designs from two-dimensional drawings and floor plans. By looking at this minia-ture set, in half-inch scale (which means that every foot of real-ity has been reduced to half inch of wood, matt board, and clay), a director can picture his blocking, a choreographer can plan the dances, a stage manager/crew chief can picture how to move the sets on and off and how big a crew they will need, the scenics can begin to plan for the paint job needed, etc.

The designer also presents a series of plans and elevations. These, done either by hand or on a computer using a drawing program (CAD—or Computer-Aided-Design program is a specialty program for architects that works well—and there are other theater-specific programs out there) show a number of details. The elevations show what the pieces and drops look like from all angles, in color, so that the technical director can build from them and the scenics can paint. This is also helpful to the costume designer in planning a color palette for the costumes. Depending on the expertise of the designer, the plans might also show exactly how to construct the set—from what type of wood to use and where the construction elements go—but often it might be left to the TD (tech director) to do a separate set of construction blue-prints and plans.

The floor plans show the director and staff exactly where the set pieces reside on the set and show the designer an overhead view of the stage and wing space—unless the theater provides him with this information, drawn by a previous designer, and he copies it for as many scenes and scene shifts that will be needed. Then he draws overhead views of each set piece, each curtain, each traveler, and so forth, placing them on the floorplan where they will be used for each scene (i.e., Act I, Scene 6, Act II, Scene 8). This enables the director to see how he can block the show, best utilizing the various sets; the lighting designer can see where to place his lighting instruments, and the shift crew/crew chief can begin to see a traffic pattern for getting the sets on and off and storing them in the wings.

If you're lucky, the designer is also an artist and will spend some time supervising the other scenics in how to paint the set to look like his model and his renderings.

Lighting Designer

While the set designer's job starts even before the show goes into rehearsals, the LD's work begins later in the production and comes to a head during tech week. During preproduction, the LD gets an inventory from the theater of available lighting instruments and peripherals, such as two-fers (which enable you to gang two instruments together), booms (to mount lights on in the wings), and maybe even a color scroller or two, which are devices that electronically change gel colors. He or she also sees if there are any special effects equipment such as hazers or smoke machines (invaluable gadgets—more on these in later chapters), mirror balls, black lights, and such. He or she researches available lighting battens and hanging positions, the amount of dimmers and their wattage, and the type of dimmer board and electrical service into the theater. While I will go into more detail on all this equipment in a later chapter, a lighting designer should have extensive knowledge of all the state-of-the-art advances in equipment, a solid education and experience with everything electrical, as well as an artistic eye.

Similar to the scenic designer, the LD utilizes floor plans, either hand drawn or using a computer with a program such as Vectorworks Spotlight, to plot out where all the lighting instruments will hang, the color gel that is put in front of the lens to color the beam of light, what dimmer and circuit each instrument is plugged into, where the light is focused, and how they might be ganged together.

This floor plan allows the master electrician and his electricians to "hang the plot"—meaning, put every instrument in its place, plug everything in, secure all the cables, put all the gels in place and do a rough focus—hopefully all before tech week.

Then the real work begins. With one or more electricians on a scaffold, ladder, or Genie Lift (a wonderful electrical device that raises a bucket high into the air) and with his hands on a light, another electrician at the dimmer board, and the LD standing on stage with either an intercom system, a walkie-talkie or a loud voice, each instrument is turned on to make sure it lights and is plugged into the proper circuit and channel. The LD then tells the electrician at the instrument exactly where to focus it, where to make the shutter cuts (metal devices inside the light that shape the beam) and whether the light beam should have hard or soft edges. They then move on to the next light, sometimes having to focus several hundred in a big theater. A daunting job indeed.

Finally, during either a cue-to-cue rehearsal (a rehearsal where the play is not performed but the actors move about from each scene change and each lighting change, holding while tweaks are made) or "on the fly" over several rehearsals, the lighting cues are perfected. Ultimately, the finished design artistically correctly reflects what lights come up on what cue and the timing of fade-ins and fade-outs.

If the theater is lucky enough to possess electronically automated cyber lights—which are lighting instruments that can actually physically move, change colors, and change gobos—these can be added during tech week for some really spectacular effects. Any lighting designer would happily take the extra time needed to program these wonderful inventions.

Another helpful computer tool for the LD is Lightwright 3 by John McKernon Software, which aids in charting the number of lighting instruments, their circuiting, their focus, their color and the like. It generates paperwork that can then be handed out to the electricians who do the work in getting all the lights set and plugged in properly and helps with troubleshooting in the event of problems.

Costume Designer

The costume designer is in charge of what everyone wears in the show and, through research and his or her own ingenious artistry, ties it all together to work well with the play itself, the set and lighting design, and the specific actors. Working with the costume shop personnel, costumes tend to come from three general sources. First, costumes can be rented. There are great costume rental houses all over the country. If you are lucky enough to be near one, you can go and pick, or "pull" as it is called, the costumes yourself that you wish to rent. Otherwise, you can tell the rental house exactly what you are looking for, and their staff pulls them, based on actor's measurements that you provide, and they ship them to you. After the show closes you ship them back. Some houses require that they are dry-cleaned first.

Second, costumes can be bought—at retail stores, thrift stores, antique stores, and tux rental houses—wherever there are clothes. Most likely a modern dress show would be bought.

Third, costumes can be pulled from the theater's stock, if they have any, and then altered or refurbished as need be.

There is a fourth way, which I do not like. The actors can be asked to supply their own costumes. If you do that, then the least the theater should do is have them dry-cleaned after the run and have any damage professionally repaired.

There is a world of difference between just making sure everyone has something to wear and designing a show with an eye for color, texture, accuracy, and creativity. Your budget and the artistry of your costume designer will determine where in this world you wind up.

Stage Manager

The stage manager in community theater is many things—a director wannabe, a production secretary, an "earth mother" to the cast, a go-fer, a collaborator, even a "bad cop" to the director's "good cop" if the need arises.

The SM attends every rehearsal and keeps the "prompt book." One way to define a prompt book might be—if in 100 years someone wanted to exactly recreate your particular show, down to the minutest details, they could do so by following the prompt book. Every bit of blocking, every prop used, every set shift is notated cleanly in the "prompt book" copy of the script.

During the tech period, the SM helps guide the various departments in coordinating the final stages of the rehearsal process. And during the show, the stage manager "calls" the show—meaning he or she sits either in the wings or in the lighting booth, script in hand, and delivers "warning" and "go" cues to the volunteer operating the lighting board, the follow spot operators, the sound board operator, and the shift crews/crew chief, whichever are applicable.

The "warning" cue, spoken over headsets, is given approximately half a page before the "go" cue, whether that "go" cue means "hit the button" that executes the lighting cue or bring up so-and-so's mic for an entrance, or push the wagon holding the set into place.

The stage manager is often an under-appreciated job in community theater—and the SM often takes the brunt of any disagreements. But a good SM keeps the production rolling, and it is indeed a valuable position to nurture.

Technical Director

The technical director (TD) at a community theater is the person who knows the most about carpentry and needs a good working knowledge of lighting, props, and sound as well, for it is the TD who makes sure everything that needs to happen technically actually happens, and in a timely fashion. If it needs to be built, flown, hung, moved, or constructed in any fashion, the TD is behind it. He or she translates the designer's plans into the language the carpenters and builders can understand—whether that is verbally or in the form of schematics and architectural plans. The TD meets with the designers upfront, plans out a schedule, and then holds weekly (ideally) production meetings with all the department heads to make sure everything is on schedule.

Sound Designer

Depending upon the theater, there may or may not be a need for a sound designer. In a small, intimate house, where sound reenforcement in the way of microphones is not needed, then someone on the lighting crew might take care of any sound effects that might be used, and perhaps another volunteer might run the tape/CD or mini-disk player. But in a large indoor or outdoor theater, where twenty or so body mics are needed in addition to floor and hanging mics for each performance, where the orchestra is individually mic'd and giant arrays of speaker clusters are needed, a sound designer might be the most important job of all. I have always found that compared to sound, all other departments have it easy. If the stage is too dark, add another light—you can see, and so you can change it. If a chair is too wobbly, reenforce it. If you don't like the color of the shirt, get another one. But sound is elusive—you can't see or feel it, and if it isn't working, it takes a real pro to fix it. So if yours is a theater where sound is an issue, I suggest you hire a pro right from the beginning. More on sound later.

Rigger

Rigging refers to the physical system that allows for hanging scenery in the theater as well as to the act of setting up such scenery. The rigger is the person who takes care of such things. Rarely is a technician dedicated to rigging—rather it falls to the tech director or to one of the electricians. Whoever handles it for your theater must understand completely what they are doing, for improper rigging is dangerous. They must know the strength and weight load of the battens and pipes they are using. If the theater has a fly system they must know how the hemp lines and weight balance system work. If they are trying to rig scenery to move on pulleys attached to the I-beams in the ceiling of the theater, they must research the practicality of such ideas. Safety should be the first concern.

I would suggest that the person in charge of rigging familiarize themselves with a company called Sapsis Rigging out of Lansdowne, Pennsylvania. Their catalog not only is a source for rigging hardware but also is full of tips. Their Internet address is: *www.sapsisrigging.com/.*

"Stage Rigging Handbook" by Jay O. Glerum, published by Southern Illinois University Press, is also a great reference.

Various Crews

I think only a word or two is necessary here. These positions will be filled with volunteers with varying experience, so your crew heads or crew chiefs will need to clearly define and explain what is expected for things to run smoothly.

Carpenters (helmed by the master carpenter)

People handy with a hammer and a screw gun are needed—choose folks who won't get hurt in the carpentry shop.

Scenic Artists (helmed by the charge scenic)

Those with artistic ability will paint the details, but people who paint the white base coats and are handy with a roller are needed as well.

Stitchers/Drapers/Cutters (helmed by the costume shop head)

Home economic students take note—here you need those folks who can mend, alter, and generally sew for hours.

Electricians (helmed by the master electrician)

While those with a working knowledge of electrics will be revered, someone needs to cut gel and hang lights and pull cable, so as long as your staff is careful around open sockets, dedication is almost as important as knowledge.

Property Artisans (propsters)

Here you need folks with imagination. Aside from those props that you can go out and purchase, props can be and often are made from the most unlikely items. Horses are made from papier-mâché; "victrolas" from cardboard; trees, from tissue paper. If you can get away with it, then get away with it. So your propsters should be masters in the art of arts and crafts.

Stage Crew (helmed by the crew chief)

The strongest will push the sets and pull the curtains and fly the scenery; the more diminutive will make sure the props are where they belong and will help dress the actors. Very important are people who will perform "hand-offs"—when an actor runs into the wings and needs to hand his prop to someone, and dressers are invaluable in those quick costume changes.

Follow Spot Operators

Not much to say here—the follow spot operators operate the follow spots, which might number one, two, four, or more. It's an art, to be sure, to smoothly follow a performer and keep the light right in the proper place (the performers eyes should be in the top third of the beam), iris in and out (make the circle larger or smaller), and execute the cues when to turn the light on and off, but with a little practice, volunteers can have a lot of fun.

Board Operator

This job can be as simple as pushing a button when told, but the best "board ops" know the show and can anticipate the cues and can also correct a mistake, such as when a cue is called too early. Of course I'm referring to computer boards when I say push a button; older theaters might have the type of board where the lights must be patched and fades are executed by pulling large levers. In that case, the job is slightly more complicated.

House Manager

The house manager is in charge of getting the people seated, making sure any special needs are met with respect to disabilities, and that the ushers and ticket people are all there, doing their jobs. If a dispute arises, the house manager runs to the rescue.

Box Office Staff, Ticket Takers, Ushers, Refreshments Sellers

The way some community theaters handle these positions is to have all of their members rotate over different performances or during different shows. Ushers and ticket takers can often be some of the youngsters in the organization, but anyone who handles money should be trusted and responsible.

Custodial Staff/Maintenance

You should be so lucky—to have a custodial staff. Sometimes even the producer has to clean the toilets. But if you can afford a cleaning service, then it would certainly be worthwhile. Maintenance to the building should fall to the tech director, who can usually fix most problems with his carpentry skills. What he can't fix will obviously have to be farmed out to a professional.

Pay strict attention now—here's a tip that can help you in every aspect of running a community theater.

Let's say you need a plumber. The first route to take is to see if you can barter for their service, and the easiest way to do that is through a reciprocal ad in your program. Throughout the years I have used this ploy for all sorts of services and products from dry cleaning to the donation of carpet remnants.

I find that when I place a phone call to a vender, and say, "Hi, I'm from such-and-such theater . . ." if I'm greeted with a "Hi! I've seen all of your shows . . . we just love you guys!" then I know the world is mine. If I get a deadpanned "Yeah, how can I help you?" I know I'm dead in the water and better be prepared to pay retail.

Office Staff

Publicists, Program Creator/Designer, Billing Department/Treasurer, People to Maintain a Website and Secure Grants

It is usually prudent, and often easy, to find people who will volunteer a few hours a week to work in "the office," whether you have an actual physical office or whether you ask them to work from their homes. Some theaters are fortunate enough to have a full- or part-time office worker/administrative assistant on the payroll. Some theaters depend on the producer or the board to handle the clerical work. Regardless of how it gets done, some of the workload includes writing and sending out or faxing or emailing press releases to the local newspapers, magazines, radio, and TV stations.

A well-written press release is some of the best publicity a theater can ask for. It opens the door to being included in the media's "weekend section," "local listings of things to do," and the like. If you include a good quality 5 by 7 black-and-white production photo or cast member's head shot, you increase your chances of getting into print, as local newspapers and news services are often hungry to fill space in their entertainment sections. With any luck, your press release will spur the paper to send someone out to do a feature story with photos, which holds more weight than an ad in the public's eye any day.

Send press releases out two to three weeks before any show dates, auditions, or special events, and send them to every paper, no matter how small you think they are, in your vicinity—it's money well spent.

Programs are major productions, particularly if you want them to bear a resemblance to "Playbills"—the professional programs of the Broadway theater. Someone needs to set these up and make them ready for a printer. You can hire a publicist to do it, but that can be expensive. Generally, it falls to someone good with a computer and adept at Microsoft Publisher or Adobe Premiere or QuarkXpress or a similar program.

A program needs to include the following:

A "title page"—with proper author credit. The licensing company (see Chapter 3) will provide this. A title page usually includes the creative and producing staff as well.

It should also include the show's logo. Logos are the artwork designed for the show and licensed for your use in promoting the show either by the licensing company or by a place called:

Package Publicity Service

27 West 24th Street, Suite 402
New York, NY 10010
212-255-2872

For a modest fee, they provide ad slicks in various sizes, production press books (a great help in writing press releases) and even posters.

Inside the program one would find a breakdown of the scenes in the show, and in the case of a musical, the songs and who sings them. The actors and their roles are also listed, and generally bios (biographies) are written for the cast and creative staff. This is most often accomplished by asking the actors and staff to fill out an informational publicity sheet, which asks for the following information:

- Name, as you would like it to appear in print
- Role or position
- Biographical information, in *XXX* words or less (substitute a number that is reasonable, based on the size of the cast/crew and the number of bios you hope to include)

- Your local town newspaper/radio station/television station (this is important because you might be able to get a feature story on a specific actor in that actor's hometown paper)

- Do you have a website and do you wish to link ours with yours? (if so, you would provide the hyper-link text and your artwork—whoever maintains your website would know how to do this)

Once this information is assembled, someone with creative writing skills might re-write the bios into a cohesive whole, making them uniform in size and style. You can also decide whether you are going to include all the little cutesy sayings that actors tend to want to close their bios with, such as: "I dedicate my performance to Rags, my Scottish Terrier. Thanks Rags, love 'ya'!"

If it is appropriate to the venue and the show, then by all means use that casual style. If not, a more formal approach can be taken.

Photos of the performers are also a nice touch; these can be taken with a digital camera at a rehearsal and brought into the computer, altered to size and corrected with a program such as Adobe Photoshop and then imported into the program you are using to design the program. You can consider also including photos from past shows, a feature article on the theater's history, and upcoming productions.

Last, it should include any special thanks to people who helped with the production but are not actively involved. The theater's staff should be listed, as well as the names of people who have made donations—whether monetary or in goods. Include information such as what "Special Need" facilities you have available, whether you have "infrared listening devices" and large-print copies of your programs. Instruct what to do in emergencies with respect to exits and list disclaimers about the taking of photographs and recording sound and video (forbidden) and beepers and cell phones (shut them off).

Remember, the program can also be a wonderful source of revenue as well. Full-page, half-page, and quarter-page ads can be sought from local venders. More often than not you can cover the printing costs of the program with revenue from advertisers alone. This takes personnel to solicit the ads and to make sure they pay in a timely fashion, but it is well worth it.

Programs are most often given out free, but a variation on the theme would be what I'll call a "souvenir program." This is often larger, both in size and in content, and printed on glossy stock and might contain many more photos, a theater's history, feature stories, and other articles. They cost a lot more to produce and are often sold for a few dollars.

Bookkeeper/Accountant/Office Manager

Someone needs to keep the books, make deposits of ticket sales, invoice advertisers, and pay the bills. Once again, this might fall to the producer or a board member, or I've seen it happen where a local accountant takes an interest in the theater and handles these jobs. Whoever handles it must, of course, be astute and trustworthy, especially around tax time.

Legalities

Many theaters apply for and receive not-for-profit status with the government. This is advantageous for a number of reasons, the most important being you do not pay taxes on items you buy. There are also other tax benefits. I am neither a tax lawyer nor an accountant, so I cannot give advice on all the ins and outs; it would do the fledgling theater well to seek professional counsel when setting up the theater's tax status for the first time or when an established theater is revisiting their financial situation. Consult a Certified Public Accountant for details.

And while we're on this legal stuff, don't forget insurance—certainly fire and theft to protect the building and all your equipment, but perhaps what is more important is liability. Actors, especially dancers, get hurt, and you want to be protected. Make sure you seek professional advice and make sure you are more than adequately covered.

And don't ever be personally legally responsible for the theater—make sure you and the board set up a corporation so that no one is personally liable. If there are lawyers and accountants involved with your group, take advantage of them, but make sure you don't mess around in the areas of taxes, insurance, liability, and corporations.

And get someone who knows how to set up the books and handle the checks. Avoid sloppy bookkeeping; it'll cause you trouble in the long run.

I know it might feel like I am mentioning all this legal stuff merely in passing, but that's because I didn't want to devote a whole chapter to something I can't speak professionally about. I'm the creative type. You need a lawyer and an accountant on board, whether they do it for free, for an ad, or for a fee. Do it right from the get-go and sleep easier at night.

A Presence on the World Wide Web

Maintaining a website is something I enjoy doing, and in this day and age I recommend it highly. The website can be simple and straightforward, or sophisticated and busy, full of flash "plug-ins" and the like. That's not really important. What *is* important is that the information be there, in a clear, easy to get to manner. Most important would be such items as schedules, directions, box office policies, and the ability to send an email from the website to the theater. Frills might include photos from your shows, links to other theater-oriented sites, history, coming attractions, a "word from the producer" on any number of subjects (I tend to change mine once a month), the ability to order tickets online (you must be able to accept charge cards), seating charts, and feature stories. The sky (and your server's capacity) is the limit, but just make sure that the info is easily accessible and download times are not excessive. Take a peak at *www.playsinthepark.com.* You'll want to purchase a Domain Name—make sure it is easily remembered and search-engine friendly. There are hundreds of companies out there who can sell you domain names as well as provide the server for your site. Use the web itself to seek out such companies.

Grants

One last important job for your office staff—securing grants. All kinds of grants are available—from local agencies like your Cultural and Heritage Commission to corporate grants (who often having matching funds—they will match a donation from an individual) to county and state grants. You never know until you try if you are eligible. Having written grant proposals from the theater's perspective and having been on a panel that reviews grants from the opposite perspective, there are a few things I've learned. First and foremost, follow the instructions the organization provides on how to submit the grant proposal. Whatever is asked for must be provided, whether it's fifteen copies of your most recent program to a notarized financial report. The review board looks most favorably on proposals that conform to the standards and guidelines they present to you. If workshops or classes are offered in how to write a grant, attend them. In fact, for one such grant that we apply for yearly, attending their workshop is mandatory. I also recommend that you present a professional package—it may sound irrelevant, but the professionally presented submission—the one that has been done immaculately on a word processor and submitted in a binder—will command more attention than a handwritten one, done on lined paper and stapled together. It's all in the presentation. Once again, use the Internet to find out what grants are available in your neck of the woods.

Onward to the next step.

Securing the Rights

You are now ready to go and choose your first play or musical. Where do you get the scripts and the scores, and who owns the rights to the show you want to produce?

In case it hadn't occurred to you, you do indeed have to secure the rights to do a show, pay royalties to the authors, rent the scripts and scores (and sometimes other rehearsal materials), and then ship all the rehearsal materials back.

And what shows can you choose from?

As much as you might want to do the latest British mega hit gracing the New York stage, there are just some shows that aren't available to amateur community theaters.

Generally speaking, you cannot produce a hit play that is still running in New York. As of this writing, *Phantom of the Opera* (the Webber version, not the Kopit version), *Les Miz*, and *The Producers* are verboten. However, when I first conceived of this book, *Miss Saigon* and *Cats* were still running. They have since closed, but the rights to them are "Restricted." Basically that means that within a certain radius to New York City they would not be available, and whereas the rights might be available outside of what is known as the tri-state area (New York, New Jersey, and Connecticut), it would depend on whether there is a First Class National Tour playing at a theater in a certain radius of your theater. My theater is currently on a waiting list for both shows—I will be advised when the tour is over—usually twelve to eighteen months.

Once a show closes in New York City, it will most likely go on the road with a First National Tour, then perhaps a Second National Tour, and then maybe a Bus and Truck tour—all produced by professionals paying heftier rights than you, as an amateur theater, would pay. The show will play the professional theaters in your town or towns next to you, sometimes known as "a booking house" in that they book in established touring shows rather than producing ones themselves. You won't be able to get the rights while these shows are "on the road." The reason behind this is that the tour might come to a professional theater in your town, or a neighboring town, and your version—with a less hefty admission charge—might steal potential patrons.

Some shows are also "restricted" when they are being revived on Broadway. Even a thirty-year-old show could be restricted if it is being mounted by professionals in a major First Class revival; therefore sometimes a moratorium will be placed on the vehicle. For example, *Joseph and the Amazing Technicolor Dreamcoat* is often restricted due to the fact that it tours professionally so often. As of this writing, there is a British redux of *Oklahoma* playing in New York City, and so that old chestnut will not be available in certain areas. *Into the Woods* is being revived on Broadway—I am aware of a college, which had the rights and planned this show, only to find those rights rescinded when the revival got the green light.

Every time a *Fiddler on the Roof* or a *Hello, Dolly!* or a *Jesus Christ, Superstar* gets a major revival in New York City, the rights are pulled in certain areas, usually thirty miles or so around New York. That's why it helps to check out websites such as Playbill OnLine (*www.playbill.com*) to see what is happening on the Great White Way.

Side note: A major exception to this was *The Fantasticks* which premiered on May 3, 1960, in its home at the Sullivan Street Playhouse, Greenwich Village, but was done constantly across the globe. The show has subsequently closed, on January 13, 2002, after 17,162 performances but was always a staple at community theaters, colleges, and high schools even while it ran in New York City.

With your permission, I would like to digress with an interesting anecdote—at least I hope you'll find it interesting. I remember back in the 1970s I brazenly recreated the script for a famous rock musical by memorizing as much of it as I could while watching the show several times on Broadway. I then asked a talented piano-playing friend of mine to transcribe the music as I wrote down the lyrics off of the original cast album, and we rehearsed at a local university while the Broadway show was thriving on the Great White Way. That particular university eventually got nervous, but another university told us that if we got permission from the New York producers we could do the show in their theater. Well, it was the time of flower power and free love, and this show was so unconventional to begin with that we actually got permission by going to the Manhattan office of the producer and begging. What we were asking was so outrageous he gave us the go ahead! But it's now 2002 and times are different—so don't try this at home—you can get sued, and sued big.

Musicals

Okay, you've given up on *The Lion King* and have settled for *South Pacific* or *The Music Man*—just how do you go about getting the rights to mount the show?

There are four organizations that hold the rights to the great majority of the major musicals ever written. They are:

Music Theater International

421 West 54th Street
New York, NY 10019
212-541-4684
Fax: 212-397-4684
licensing@mtishows.com
http://www.mtishows.com

Tams-Witmark Music Library

560 Lexington Avenue
New York, NY 10022
212-688-2525
Fax: 212-688-3232
http://www.tams-witmark.com/musical.html

Samuel French House of Plays and Musicals

45 West 25th Street
New York, NY 10010-2751
212-206-8990

Fax: 212-206-1429
Musical Department—212-206-8125
or
7623 Sunset Blvd.
Hollywood, CA 90046-2795
213-876-0570
Fax: 213-876-6822

The Rodgers and Hammerstein Theatre Library
229 West 28th Street
11th Floor
New York, NY 10001
212-564-4000
Fax: 212-268-1245
http://www.rnh.com

All offer perusal copies of the scripts, and some offer loaners of the scores—although there sometimes is a fee for this. You get to keep the material for about ten days to two weeks to decide if it is the show for you, then you have to mail it back. Photocopying the librettos and scores is illegal—it is all copyrighted.

"MTI" (Music Theater International) handles most of Stephen Sondheim's shows, Bock and Harnick's shows, and classics such as *The Fantasticks*. They are a well-organized operation and provide a lot of support materials. They have midi files of the music for you to rehearse with, which you receive on floppy disks for either IBM or Mac computers. They even have the software for a free midi player that comes on the disk! They offer director guides as well as video interviews with the authors of many of their shows. They will sell you the original cast CDs and carry alternate versions of the orchestrations to suit varying needs. These "reductions," as they are called, are done by professionals, so instead of just eliminating players, you get a new version of the score, orchestrated for fewer instruments. This is an excellent way to go if you do musicals and cannot house or afford a full eighteen- to twenty-two-piece orchestra. Please note that MTI is not the only one to offer orchestral reductions for some of their shows.

Live musicians can be a daunting and expensive proposition, but nothing makes a musical more professional than a large, wonderful sounding orchestra. If, however, you have to reduce a score that called originally for twenty-three sidemen (a musician other than the conductor) to eight or nine players, it would sound empty if you merely discarded the books (orchestra parts) for fourteen or fifteen of the remaining players. It is not an easy task to decide if Reed 4 is dispensable, or if you could lose the entire string section or one of the percussionists. This is why a "reduced orchestration" is such a good thing—it is a professionally cutdown version, often rewriting violin and harp parts, for instance, for a keyboardist to play. If you must reduce the number of players significantly, always inquire if there is a reduced orchestration available.

MTI also has a terrific website—*www.mtishows.com*, and a great brochure, that lists the cast and set requirements and gives you the orchestra breakdown.

Tams-Witmark handles a lot of Jerry Herman's musicals and some of the big classic musicals such as *Cabaret, My Fair Lady*, and even *You're A Good Man, Charlie Brown* (both the new and the old version!). They have a colorful brochure that comes out often and also have reduced orchestrations for some of their shows. Not all the orchestrations are listed for every show in their catalog, but a call to their music "librarian" with inquiries should answer most of your questions as to how the show is scored. Or try their website—*http://www.tamswitmark.com/musical.html*.

R&H—Rodgers and Hammerstein Theatre Library—handle, you guessed it, all the Rodgers and Hammerstein musicals. In addition, they have works by Rodgers and Hart, Kurt Weill, Irving Berlin, and a few other shows such as *Big River, Once Upon A Mattress*, and *Show Boat*. They carry a lot of the oldies but goodies. Many of their shows—since they are from days gone by in terms of musical theater—have huge orchestra requirements.

However, they recently secured the rights to the whole Andrew Lloyd Webber catalog, and so you would now use them for *Joseph and the Amazing Technicolor Dreamcoat, Jesus Christ, Superstar, Song and Dance*, as well as *Cats*, when available. There is still no word, however, on *Sunset Boulevard* as of this writing.

Last, there's French (Samuel French House of Plays). French is also a licensing house for straight plays (nonmusicals), but they do have a extensive musical library containing such well-sought-after shows as *Grease, The Secret Garden, Best Little Whorehouse in Texas* (a big seller if you can get away with the title), *Falsettos*, and the non-Andrew Lloyd Webber version of *The Phantom of the Opera* entitled *Phantom*. They offer a separate brochure called "Musicals from the House of Plays." The orchestral requirements are listed in this catalog. French tends to sell the playscripts outright—you'll need to buy all the copies from them—and then they rent you the scores for a month or two.

All of the previously cited companies rent you the rehearsal material. It is not for sale, although sometimes the piano conductor scores can be bought in big bookstores or online for about $75.00. Try Colony Records (212-265-2050) in New York City for a large assortment of scores and individual sheet music of Broadway songs.

When licensing a show, you usually get the scripts two months before your opening night and the scores one month before you open (musicians rehearse less), but you can pay extra for extending that time frame. You can also request more copies of scripts or orchestra parts than are provided in the basic package of rehearsal material for additional money as well.

Costs involved in leasing a musical can vary dramatically. Usually they are based on the popularity of the show, the amount of seats your theater holds, your scale of ticket prices, and the number of performances. You usually pay a rental fee for the rehearsal material, a fee for the first performance, and a lesser fee for each subsequent performance. Sometimes you can haggle a bit, especially if you agree to sell fewer seats. It doesn't hurt to ask.

They will quote you the costs if you send or fax a written application with your dates, ticket prices, seating capacity, etc. You can also use the websites.

Most of these houses also handle musical revues (compilations of a composer's work or an evening of songs held together by a theme, such as *Side by Side By Sondheim* or *The World Goes 'Round*—which is made up of the Kander and Ebb library of show tunes.) These are often easier to mount than a full musical and can flesh out a theater's season with an easy yet popular musical-style offering.

Children's musicals are also available from these companies. I love the Prince St. Players' shows handled by MTI. Many carry specialty shows for holidays such as various versions of *A Christmas Carol* or Meredith Wilson's adaptation of *Miracle on 34th Street* called *Here's Love*.

You can also get Gilbert and Sullivan shows. Now you might question why, if these shows are in the public domain, would we have to pay for rights? What you are primarily paying for is the version of the orchestrations you are getting, or in the case of *Pirates of Penzance*—the Joe Papp version—you are paying for the right to use all the changes and updates that were made to the piece.

As an added bonus: some of the leasing houses, MTI and French especially, will sell you posters and logos (those adorable little drawings that represent the show, such as George Bernard Shaw controlling the marionettes of Henry Higgins and Eliza Doolittle associated with—Okay, for 10 points, which show?). You can use these as the cover art for your playbills and other publicity. I like to scan them in my computer and paste them on to cast lists and press releases—very impressive! I mentioned earlier, but it bears repeating, a wonderful organization in New York City called Package Publicity Service (212-255-2874) that sells the logos as ad slicks in varying sizes (ready to be photocopied or scanned), booklets containing background information, and reviews of the musicals and plays, postcards, posters—a whole wealth of research and publicity material.

Your best bet is to get on the websites or the phone and request the catalogs. Very quickly you'll be up to speed on who handles what.

Comedies and Dramas: Straight Plays

There are three companies handling almost all the major plays.

Samuel French House of Plays and Musicals, mentioned previously, handles loads of straight plays, as do:

Dramatist Play Service

440 Park Avenue South
New York, NY 10016
212-683-8960
Fax: 212-213-1539
email: *postmaster@dramatists.com*
www.dramatists.com

The Dramatic Publishing Company

PO Box 129
Woodstock, IL 60098
800-448-7469
www.dramaticpublishing.com

Their catalogs are great and very helpful. They list the plays in all sorts of ways, including: by author, by number of characters, by scenic demands, whether it is suitable for children, teenagers, colleges or adults . . . the list goes on. You can find the right show for all your specifics.

Licensing a straight play is significantly easier than a musical. Usually there is only one author, rather than a book writer, composer and lyricist, so you are not paying a lot of different royalties. The cost doesn't vary much. It is usually a set fee no matter the size of your house for the first performance, and then a fee for each subsequent performance. Nice and clean and easy. And since you buy the scripts, you don't have to return anything. No rental fees.

Every theater should keep copies of the catalogs from all licensing companies and each year request their newest version. They are invaluable.

Legal Requirements

There are a few legal things you need to do, which is true of musicals as well, in terms of the credit given the authors and the leasing company.

Generally, your program and posters need to include the author's name(s) in a certain typeface and size, based on the typeface and size of the font you use for the title. You also need to include the phrase "Produced by special arrangement with" and then the name MTI, Tams Witmark, or Samuel French, as the case may be. This is all spelled out in your contract.

An example of your program's title page might be:

Rodgers & Hammerstein's	75%
THE KING & I	100%
Music by RICHARD RODGERS	75%*
Book and Lyrics by OSCAR HAMMERSTEIN II	75%*
Based on "Anna and the King of Siam" by	
Margaret Landon	45%
Original Choreography by Jerome Robbins	56¼%

---

* Immediately following the title and in no event less than that of the largest, most prominent credit given to any other person.

(Yes, you read correctly—fifty-six and one-quarter percent for Mr. Robbins!)

The previous is lifted right from the contract I have for *The King & I* with R&H. That means if you have an actress playing Anna who demands over the title billing, it will affect everyone and everything else!

Then you must also include:

THE KING & I is presented through special arrangement with The Rodgers and Hammerstein Theatre Library, 229 West 28th Street, 11th Floor, New York, NY 10001

The previous can be confusing, so let me add this clarification. You start with the title, *The King and I*, and choose a style and size of typeface font. This is the font size that governs the size of all the other credits.

If you choose the title to look like this:

THE KING AND I

which happens to be the typeface Impact in a 22-point font size, this would dictate that the credit "Music by Richard Rodgers" would be 75 percent of the title's size. In other words, the 100 percent refers to the size of the lettering of the title of the show, which one assumes would be the biggest thing on your title page or cover. Unless, of course, you have Nathan Lane guest starring in your production—then you certainly don't need to be reading this book.

Another legal consideration is the subject of cuts and additions. This is tricky. The licensing company, on behalf of the authors, understands that you might not successfully be able to fill the entire 120 measures of a dance break that the original Broadway production managed to utilize. So cuts in the material are allowed. You may cut parts of the script or score due to time restraints, budget restraints, or talent restraints. Just use a soft pencil if marking cuts in a rented script or score.

BUT you cannot add or substitute. You cannot rearrange an orchestration. You cannot tamper with the work except to make it shorter. Even though you might like the dance breaks used in "The House of Marcus Lycus" from the recent revival of *A Funny*

Thing . . . Forum better than the ones used in the Zero Mostel version (which is what you get when you license the show), you cannot have your very talented musical director take said dance breaks from off the recording and notate it for your production. These orchestrations belong to another orchestrator who has not made them available for amateur theaters. Trust me, I asked.

So be very careful what you try to get away with. If caught, you will certainly have the rights revoked, and more serious charges could occur.

Other Companies

There are a number of smaller companies that publish lesser-known plays that are often perfect for community theaters. Baker's Plays and Pioneer Drama Service are two of the biggest:

Baker's Plays

Mail orders:
Baker's Plays
PO Box 699222
Quincy, MA 02269-9222

Reading room and store (not for any mail):
1445 Hancock Street
Quincy Center
Quincy, MA 02169
617-745-0805
Fax: 617-745-9891
www.bakersplays.com

Their catalog not only lists plays but also is a good resource for other needed goods and services such as make-up. Send for their catalog.

Pioneer Drama Service

PO Box 4267
Englewood, CO 80155-4267
1-800-33DRAMA (1-800-333-7262)
www.pioneerdrama.com

They have a great website and offer extra services and fun links to other websites. Like Baker's, they have one-act plays and melodramas, plays for young audiences, and holiday shows.

There are several smaller companies, some specializing in religious plays or plays for elementary schools—a search on the Internet will ferret them out.

If you wish to buy playscripts, either for your own library or to see if the show is one you would like to produce, The Drama Book Shop in New York is a great source for any scripts and scores that are published for sale—

The Drama Book Shop, Inc.

250 West 40th (between 7th and 8th Avenues)
New York, NY 10018

Mon.–Fri. 10 A.M.–8 P.M. EST
Sat. 10:30 A.M.–8:30 P.M. EST
Sun. noon–6 P.M. EST

212-944-0595
800-322-0595
Fax: 212-921-2013

Also, Stage and Screen (formerly Fireside Theater) is a mail-order book club that handles hardcover versions of some musicals and plays at a discount and is great for collectors. Visit *www.stagenscreen.com*.

Planning a Season

Let's get down to the business of producing an entire season of plays and musicals. Whether it is your first season or your seventeenth, there are a great many benefits to planning and announcing an entire season at a time, and announcing it several months in advance.

I have known theaters that announce only one or two of their shows at a time—often because they don't know what they are going to do next—and this results in a confused audience. Certainly it hurts the sale of "season tickets," a device that offers the ticket buyer an opportunity to get a ticket to one show free by buying in advance tickets to the whole season. Along those same lines, it is inadvisable to cancel or change a show midseason, as that also makes for poor public relations.

So a lot of careful thought must go in to selecting shows— there are scores of variables to consider.

Just for the fun of it, let's make up a season for a fictitious community theater. We'll call our theater the Amityville Community Theater. Our theater produces two musicals and two straight plays each season, and a season is from October through May (we're not air conditioned, so we don't run over the summer). Each of our shows play for twelve performances over three weekends each— Thursday, Friday, and Saturday nights at 8 P.M. and Sunday matinee at 2 P.M. If a theater group wishes to buy out an entire evening, and if we know in sufficient time to plan and secure the actors, we will run a special Wednesday night show, Sunday night show, or a Saturday matinee. We usually can count one of these for each of the four shows, and we tell our actors to plan for this at auditions.

Our pool of talent is fairly consistent—since our shows are of good quality and well received we can count on a core of about thirty-five to fifty regulars auditioning, and depending on the show, we might pull another twenty-five if we do a very popular title. There are two other community theaters about a twenty-minute drive from our theater in opposite directions, and so it isn't always a breeze to cast every show. Therefore one of our considerations has to be—can we cast the four shows we wish to do?

Casting the Season

Let's look at musicals first, since they require the largest number of participants, and the performers not only have to act, but sing and dance as well. This lowers the number of people auditioning somewhat.

We might break down our requirements into categories—leads, supporting characters, and ensemble.

The supporting characters are the easiest to cast in any musical—often these are roles that require only minimal dancing and singing abilities—actors who more often than not generally try out for only the straight plays might be able to fill some of these supporting roles.

To give but a few examples: Cigar, the owner of the strip joint in *Gypsy*; Mr. Bratt, an executive in *How to Succeed . . .* ; Smee in *Peter Pan*; Ernst Ludwig in *Cabaret;* and Col. Pickering in *My Fair Lady*. These juicy and fun roles are primarily acting roles—requiring character actors, who can often "talk-sing" whatever songs they are included in.

But the leads and the ensemble are a different story. Whereas most theaters pride themselves on "open casting" and not "pre-casting" any roles, it would be foolhardy to plan on a musical that was written as a star vehicle without having at least one person in your stables that can handle the role.

First, a definition of star vehicle, then some words on pre-casting. By a star vehicle, I'm referring to a musical in which a performer with name recognition has traditionally played the leading character in professional theater. The roles not only require extraordinary talent but also larger than life personae. Such roles include Tevye in *Fiddler*, Harold Hill in *The Music Man*,

Mame and Vera in *Mame*, Dolly in *Hello, Dolly!*, Mama Rose in *Gypsy*, Don Quixote in *Man of La Mancha*, Charity in *Sweet Charity* (in fact, when the name of the show is the name of the main character you can more or less assume a star was in the original.), Evita in *Evita* (see what I mean?).

This is opposed to shows where the leads are either more or less equal or there are a number of them to carry the load in ensemble fashion, such as *1776, Into the Woods, Company, Working, The Fantasticks, Damn Yankees, Guys and Dolls, The Pajama Game, She Loves Me*.

Unless your stable of reliable and dedicated performers can support it, it would be unwise to plan *Mame, Hello, Dolly!* and *Gypsy* in the same year—it is just too hard to cast the title roles. Any actress capable of really pulling off Mame Dennis could also be considered possibly for Dolly Levi or Mama Rose, and you just can't count on someone giving up what might equal four months of his or her lives for your community theater. And even if they would star in all three shows, you must consider if your audience wants to see the same actress in three major leads in the same season. She had better be pretty spectacular.

The ensemble for a musical is also a very tough nut to crack. There's a stigma attached to ensembles (which is why we call them "ensembles" rather than the more demeaning "chorus roles") that prevents a lot of performers from being in them, which is a shame, since they can be a whole lot of fun and very satisfying.

In an ideal world, your ensemble would be made up of triple threats—performers who are equally adept at acting, singing, and dancing. On Broadway, ensembles are indeed made up of triple threats, because the performers are being paid to be in the ensemble, and there's always the hope of being discovered.

In community theater, the triple threats usually demand leading roles and you are very lucky indeed to coerce them into the ensemble.

More often than not, you try for a handful of performers who can sing and carry the vocal demands of the ensemble and for a handful that can dance to carry the choreography. The dancers tend to be female, on the younger side, since they are the ones in the local dance schools. This is acceptable in ensembles that can get away with younger girls—*Music Man* and *Anything Goes* come to mind. But what do you do when presenting *Guys and*

Dolls, which demands, for "The Crapshooter Ballet," character men who can dance, or of *Hello, Dolly!*, which demands, for "The Waiter's Galop," dancing waiters?

Cross your fingers and hope that at least energetic and willing men turn out, and that you have a choreographer adept at that community theater miracle of miracles—"getting the men to look good."

This is an art in itself, and it's where a choreographer can take great pride—having a vocabulary of dance steps that she can eventually teach most men and that actually look good on them when they execute the steps.

The point of all this is to consider every casting angle when deciding on a season, making sure your choices are significantly varied as to not tax your base of known performers. There's always the hope—and supreme delight—when people come out of the woodwork for a specific show—but counting on that would be unwise.

Precasting

What about precasting? This is of constant debate among members of community theaters. You can see postings on theater message boards on the Internet and overhear angry conversations at auditions when precasting is suspected.

While I won't debate whether precasting is a fair or right choice, I will say this—being dishonest about it is a decidedly wrong choice.

If you have indeed precast an actor in one of your shows, then the only fair and decent thing to do is state this fact before auditions—in all press releases and anywhere auditions are announced. Go on record that the role of such-and-such has been cast and therefore we are not auditioning for that role. To do anything less is shabby.

I do feel there is a danger in precasting—other than turning people off—and that is the danger of limiting yourself.

Time for a short anecdote: in 1985 I directed a production of *Sweeney Todd* at a small theater with a close friend of mine playing Sweeney, and he was indeed good. The following year I was hired to direct the show again, this time at Plays-in-the-Park, where I make my theatrical home. While certainly not offering a carved-in-stone promise, my friend and I did feel that he was a shoe-in for repeating the role.

Now Plays-in-the-Park is on a much grander scale than where I first directed *Todd*, and during the audition process scores of talented people turned out. My friend auditioned, and auditioned well, but along came a fellow whose presence, voice, and delivery was so much stronger that I had no choice but to go with him to fill the huge stage that is PIP.

Had I announced that the role had been cast before auditions, I might never have met this other gifted performer. So consider every angle when considering precasting.

Technical Considerations

It also makes sense to consider the technical elements of sets, costumes, and lighting when planning your season.

We already discussed that costumes are often rented, built, or purchased. This can amount to a serious dent in your budget if you do too many "period pieces" in the same season. Trying to costume *Amadeus, Dangerous Liaisons,* a Shakespearean play, and *Guys and Dolls* all in the same season might result in most of your resources being spent on costuming! Peppering the season with a modern-day straight play can help enormously in stretching your costume budget.

The same thing applies for sets. If you plan well, you might be able to use the same flats that make up the walls of that interior living room for one straight play in such a way as to reuse them for another set—change the paint job or rearrange the location of the doors, windows, and walls. If you plan a show that takes place in an exterior as well as an interior you might not have as much construction for the exterior locale. Doing one "wing and border" musical in a season along with one that has only a single stationary set demand might also save some money and energy. A "wing and border" show refers to those old-fashioned musicals where one scene involving a big set (such as Vandergelder's Feed and Seed store in *Dolly!*) is followed by a scene played in front of a drop "in one"—which refers to the downstage set of wings—while you change to the next big set—Irene Molloy's Hat Shoppe. So on and so forth.

With respect to lighting, it's not so much choosing a season to reduce lighting demands as it is to exercise careful planning once the season is set to make the overall job easier.

If you take your four shows and find any common elements, such as the need for a "blue wash" for night scenes, or a downstage-center "special," then you could sit with your designers pre-season and come up with a "rep plot" (repertory plot). A rep plot takes a look at each lighting position—on stage, front of house, booms, cyc lights, and X-rays (strip lights)—and determines what common denominators exist for the shows. It then assigns a position for an instrument to more or less permanently be mounted (at least for the season), as well as what circuit to cable it and what dimmer to plug it in to.

In fact, most professional theaters that book in road shows utilize rep plots. You can change the color medium (gel) and re-focus any of the instruments, but you cannot change their position or circuit or channel of usually about eighty percent of the instruments. The remaining twenty percent are available to put where you want for specials.

This minimizes the time it takes to do "change-overs"—the time between shows needed to hang and cable different lighting plots. If all you have to do is re-focus and re-color the great majority of the lighting instruments then a great deal of time and personnel is reduced.

I highly recommend getting the advice of an ace lighting designer and coming up with a rep plot—it is a one-time fee that will repay itself many times over season after season. And you can always revisit the rep plot if you find yourself with new instruments or other equipment.

Getting the Audience into the Theater

Last, there's the element of attracting an audience and presenting a varied menu for even the most jaded among them. If you are in an area where there are a lot of community theaters, then you need to be careful when resurrecting an old chestnut that has been done to death—by your competition and by your theater itself. Resurrecting *Grease* for the third time in ten years will not endear you to your audience, especially when the local high school, junior school, college, and other local theaters all did it in recent memory.

But there's a catch-22 involved. You don't want to repeat all the old shows that have been done to death, but audiences rarely come out in droves for a show they have never heard of.

It's a very real problem. They've seen *The Odd Couple* to death, but never heard of *Good*—a very strong semi-musical about the rise of Nazi Germany. They are liable not to come out for either.

I have often used the old adage attached to a wedding— "Something Old, Something New, Something Borrowed, Something Blue"—although I admit to stretching it a bit to fit.

Your first show could indeed be an old favorite, just one not done recently at your theater—anything from *Oklahoma* to *Shenandoah*, from *Brighton Beach Memoirs* to *Arsenic and Old Lace*. The choices of "something old" are nearly endless.

You would next want to do a show that you have not done before, perhaps something that has closed recently on Broadway and is now available. You can take the "something new" to mean either something new to your theater, whether an older show or not, or something new in terms of recent. Perhaps this is the slot to do a musical review, or a staged reading, something that is new to the audience in terms of style.

Now here's where I'm stretching it—the "borrowed" refers to a show that you can "reinvent." When approaching a show from a director's standpoint—you can try as best you can to recreate the feeling of the original production, or you can come up with a radical new version of the show. Assuming you are still adhering to all copyright laws concerning the original script, reinventing a show might involve a change in locale or time period. Doing a modern day version of a Shakespearean play is a good example. I once heard of a production of *Company* that was set in a New York City subway rather than in the "high-rise apartments" of the original. You are "borrowing" the basic concept of the original and mixing in some new twist. It makes the show fresh for the audience and gives you a publicity angle to explore.

Last, the "blue." Stretching "blue" as far as I can, here is where you might offer the audience something out of the ordinary, perhaps something a tad more mature in nature. As long as you advertise it as such—along the lines of "viewer discretion is advised"— here is the slot for an *Equus* or *Hot L Baltimore* or anything by David Mamet. Perhaps, by producing something rarely attempted due to its mature or intellectual content, this is the chance to try and elevate the level of community theater in your area.

By presenting a season of the sort of diversity mentioned in the previous, you stand the chance of attracting a large and more varied audience.

Surveys

Speaking of your audience, demographics play an important role, and every few seasons or so it doesn't hurt to run a survey. You can do it by handing out flyers during shows with a drop-off box for replies. You can make the survey part of the program and have people fax it to you. Or you can do it on your website, with people filling in the answers online.

You might ask some of the following questions: male/female, age range, are you a subscriber, or do you attend individual shows per your liking, favorite shows at the theater the past few seasons, shows you'd like to see done—anything to give you an idea if you are on the right track.

You can't pander to the audience totally, you need to stick to your MISSION STATEMENT and I like to think it is part of a community theater's job to educate an audience to new ideas.

When I felt the audience has rejected a new and daring show I wanted to produce, I have used my "word from the producer" in the program and on the website to retaliate—gently, of course. I have stated on a number of occasions: "Hey, look, you liked shows A, B, and C. The same creative staff is responsible for show D. Chances are, therefore, that you should give D a chance—it just might surprise you."

You need to build audience awareness and audience confidence. I have found that you can't delve too quickly into uncharted waters. Give them familiar shows done well in the beginning and slowly introduce the offbeat and the experimental. You might even consider discounting the ticket price for a show that no one is familiar with or offering it as an added bonus in addition to your regular subscription season. Make it a fifth show, at the end of the season—free to subscribers for a limited run. You can always extend it if it is a hit. Eventually the audience will come to accept the variety that you offer them.

Auditions

Now that you've decided on your shows and you have your directors and designers in place, you need to turn your focus to casting and auditions. I have always felt that if you do your job properly during auditions, half the battle of mounting a show has been won. Here are my thoughts on the audition process.

Getting the Word Out

Let the community know of your upcoming auditions. Send audition notices to the local papers three weeks in advance of your audition dates. Some papers have a weekly audition column and need the information in advance, but too far in advance will result in it getting misplaced or ignored. Post your information on your website. Send out flyers to your mailing list to arrive two weeks prior to auditions.

A mailing list is a great tool for community theaters. It is a reasonably inexpensive way to reach people who are actually interested in your "product," and if you use bulk mailing it is especially inexpensive.

If you have at least 200 pieces of mail in one zip code, you can qualify for bulk mailing with the post office. Their rules change almost yearly, so please check with them. Basically, you have to sort your mail according to zip codes, bundle them according to Post Office specifics, and deliver them together to the post office—thus saving anywhere from twenty-five to thirty-five percent off the cost of a stamp. At my theater we send over 10,000 pieces and it takes us a few days to get it together, but the savings are worthwhile. Once every few years, however, we do the mailing first class just to weed out dead letters. You don't get undeliverable mail back to you when you do it bulk.

We send out a mailing prior to auditions, once in the Fall announcing our winter season and once in the Spring touting our summer season.

Regarding auditions, we at PIP do things a tad differently. We hold one major audition for all of our summer shows at one time. This is necessary since they go into rehearsal within two weeks of each other and it would be impossible to schedule individual calls for each show. Most "straw hat" theaters (a term synonymous with Summer Stock) have one huge audition in the Spring.

If you could plan in advance all your audition dates then you could reduce the number of mailings. It is not advisable, however, to send only one press release to the newspapers and magazines with a whole year's worth of auditions—they require separate ones for each a week or so in advance of each date.

Be very specific in your requirements and needs when advertising your auditions.

Here is an example of what you might send to the local newspapers, magazines, and radio/television/cable stations for *Hello, Dolly!*

AUDITIONS ANNOUNCED

Open calls announced for a production of Jerry Herman's classic musical *Hello, Dolly!* at the Barn Theater, 18 Theatrical Way, Shubert, NJ 08734.
Sunday, September 17 at 1 P.M.
Monday, September 18 at 7 P.M.
Tuesday, September 19 at 7 P.M.
Check out our website at *www.barntheater.com* for directions.
All roles are open.
Auditions are first come, first served.
Those auditioning should come prepared with the best 32 bars of an up-tempo show tune. Song does not have to be from *Hello, Dolly!* but should have similar feel. Bring your own sheet music in the proper key. An accompanist will be provided; we discourage singing either accapella or to a tape, as this does not present you in the best light.

Callbacks will be held the following weekend. If you are given a callback you will be asked to read from the script and will be taught a dance combination, so bring appropriate shoes and clothes. Sides (scenes) will be distributed at the callback; please do not call the theater asking for scripts in advance. You may also be asked to sing further from material provided to you at the callback.

You might wish to add the following to your website or mailing list audition notices:

A brief description of the roles follow:

DOLLY LEVI—larger-than-life middle-aged woman with great comic timing and a strong character voice.

HORACE VANDERGELDER—blustery and cranky middle-aged man, good comic timing, strong character voice.

CORNELIUS HACKL—early 20s, energetic, good comic timing, strong baritone voice.

BARNABY TUCKER—late teens, small, good comic timing, needs strong dance ability, strong tenor vocal range.

IRENE MOLLOY—pretty, mid to late 20s, strong lyric soprano.

MINNIE FAYE—late teens, early 20s, funny with a screechy voice, needs good dance abilities and strong alto voice.

ENSEMBLE
20 men and 20 women of varying ages and sizes, all with strong voice and excellent dance ability. Will double into supporting characters.

Not every paper will print all of this (certainly they won't print the cast breakdown), but it is indicative of the type of notice to be sent to the media, and the extended version can be displayed on your website, in mailings, and posted in the lobby of the theater.

If you were auditioning for a nonmusical you would adapt
what you expect of those auditioning. Some suggestions include:

- Ask to hear a memorized two-minute monologue.

- Allow people to pick up sides from the show prior to auditions and read them from the play with a stage manager
reading with them.

- Ask men to come at a certain time and women at another
to judge them against each other, or mix them up and
have them read with each other, two or three at a time.

- Some theaters schedule ten- or fifteen-minute slots for
auditions and you must phone for an appointment. I
find that unless you are following strict Equity rules, this
idea doesn't always work. Amateurs are not used to
showing up at precise times and your schedule will
quickly disintegrate.

- After someone sings or reads at the open call, as the case
may be, many theaters then hand the actor auditioning a
sheet that breaks down the callbacks.

It might read something like this:

Congratulations!

You are being called back for the role of _____
in *Hello, Dolly!*. Please come to the theater on Saturday,
September 22, at 2 P.M. Bring comfortable shoes you can
dance in. You will be given sections of the script to read
when you arrive. Please be prompt. The callback will last
approximately two hours.

Open and Closed Auditions

The physical structure of the audition process can take many
forms. The two most obvious—and heatedly debated—would be the
open audition and the closed audition. Sometimes things are best
understood when described by example, so here is what I prefer.

I tend to like the initial open call to be closed. The director
(with the choreographer, stage manager, and musical director if
appropriate) sits at a table at one end of the room. If it is a singing

audition, there is, of course, a piano and a piano player in the middle of the room.

Those auditioning wait in the hallway and dressing rooms (or lobby if applicable). When they arrive, they are greeted by a volunteer, who gives them a card to fill out. The card has been prenumbered, and they are handed out in the order people arrive, or at least approach.

The card requests the following information (and requests that it be written legibly—you'd be surprised!):

Name

Street Address

City, State, Zip

Home phone

Work phone

Cell phone

Email

Age

Height

Hair color

Vocal range

Dance training

Special skills

Prior experience (experienced auditioners will provide a picture and resume)

Conflicts

This last item is an extremely emotional one for me. There is NOTHING more frustrating than having a rehearsal planned and finding two or more of your principals not showing up. It is doubly frustrating because it can be avoided.

All it takes is honesty, but that's hard to impress upon someone auditioning who thinks that if they list a conflict they won't be cast.

That's just not true. Generally speaking, while I know in advance what days I am rehearsing, I hold off deciding just what specifically I will do on a given day until I check people's conflicts.

So I post my rehearsal days—say, Monday through Thursday, 7:30 to 10 P.M., and Sunday from 1 to 6 P.M., and ask that people list their known conflicts for this chunk of time: voice lessons, dance lessons, a Bar Mitzvah, whatever.

If I get honest replies and still want that particular actor, I can schedule around them. But if I don't get honesty, then anger ensues.

Okay, so the actor has filled out his card. He then waits his turn until his number is called. When his number is called, he then meets with another volunteer who collects his card and picture and resume and is instructed to give his sheet music to the accompanist if it is a musical, or just go to the middle of the room if it is a straight play. Sometimes I even put an X on the spot on the stage or the room where I want the actor to stand—usually the spot where the light is the best.

He or she confers with the piano player if it is a musical audition—we always allow a few moments for consultation, and then the performer states their name and what they are going to sing, if applicable, or what monologue they are going to read, or they await instructions from us.

This is called a "closed" audition because the other people auditioning do not watch it. So it is a "closed" open call.

When they are done, hopefully, we give them the callback sheet. If not, it is always an awkward moment when you have to say "Thank you" and not invite them to a callback. But if you are gentle and kind and offer some sort of explanation, you can often soften the blow: "I'm afraid we don't see you being right (or maybe "you are too young") for any of the roles this season, but we enjoyed your audition and hope that you will continue to audition for us in seasons to come."

Some theaters avoid this confrontation by not giving out callback notices at the open call, but rather they will make phone calls the next day alerting those who need to come to further auditions.

It is a fact of life that very few actors get the roles they audition for, and if they are to pursue theater as either a profession or a hobby they have to get used to it. If directors are sympathetic and understanding, there is nothing to feel guilty about when turning someone down.

Now let's suppose you saw 100 people at the open call for the 30 roles you are looking for and you find you have called back

60. Some preparation must go into organizing the callbacks, which I tend to have open, as opposed to closed.

Callbacks

To prepare, you must do the following: From your notes, figure out exactly who is coming back and how many people you have returning for each role. Make up a handwritten chart, or put your information into a computerized database (I like Excel) so you can manipulate the data—arranging it by audition numbers, last names, or roles.

If you are auditioning a straight play, then you must plan what scenes the auditioners are going to read. Invariably, too long a scene is chosen. You can quite quickly tell who can cut it and who can't, and if the scene is too long, it is uncomfortable in the hands of less-than-talented actors. Better to have a back-up scene if you want to hear more. A page in length is just about right.

You will want to have scenes for all the major and supporting characters. It is helpful to pair people up, especially if they interact a lot. In *Our Town,* for example, you might read the young lovers together, the two sets of parents together, and the character of the Stage Manager by himself, with a monologue.

If a minor character has a line in the middle, you can simply cross it out. Sometimes I will have supporting characters read the principal's dialogues and monologues. There are several benefits to this: fewer different scenes to deal with, the principal scenes are often more meaty, someone you considered only in support might surprise you, if they give an intelligent reading you will be able to see past the point that they are not reading for the role in the scene.

If you are auditioning for a musical, you still do the aforementioned, plus your musical director must prepare sixteen to thirty-two bars (measures) of the songs the characters sing, choosing portions that show off the vocal needs best. Often this involves the ending, which contains what we call the "money notes"—those belty, high notes that force the audience to applaud.

We usually choose one ensemble song—say "Put on Your Sunday Clothes" when auditioning *Hello, Dolly!* and have the ensemble learn sixteen bars of a section that has harmony, having them sing their specific vocal part—alto, soprano, baritone, tenor, etc.

Your choreographer must prepare a dance combination. He or she will choose a section of music that allows for movement. Choreographers often use counts in teaching a dance, whereas the pianist will be concerned with the measures in the score. It takes a meeting of the minds to create a common language, but it works out.

A choreographer will count 1,2,3,4,5,6,7,8—2,2,3,4,5,6,7,8—3,2,3,4,5,6,7,8—4,2,3,4,5,6,7,8, etc. This way they can say to fall back on your left leg on the count of "one" in the second count of eight, to give a simple example.

For an audition combination, choreographers will sometimes choose four counts of eight and have the pianist convert that to measures. Then the choreographer will fill those counts with as much as she can in the style of the show you are doing—tap for *Crazy for You* or *42nd Street,* Fosse-style jazz for *Sweet Charity* or *Pippin,* ballet for many of the R&H shows—whatever is applicable. The combination is designed to see not only who is trained and has the dance language but also who can execute the steps with style. Some people can fake it with such panache that they can get away with cheating the steps, whereas some others can do a time step accurately but without any style at all.

If the show has a number of styles, more than one combination may be necessary.

Once you are prepared with material, a little planning in executing the callback helps as well in getting the most mileage out of the time you have. After all, callbacks are generally speaking your last chance to make decisions, so you want to make sure you have seen all you need to see.

It also helps to videotape the callbacks for study later. Equity, the actor's union, will not allow you to do this, but there aren't any rules in community theater. It is polite, however, to tell the performers up front that you are videotaping, and it is for review purposes only.

Here's how a sample callback audition might be run.

Everyone assembles in a main room or on stage. Everyone will be able to watch everyone else's auditions—hence the term "open audition." Please note: the term "open audition" in this instance refers to the fact that everyone auditioning sees everyone auditioning. It is not to be confused with an "open call" at which anyone can audition, whether they are Equity or non-Equity, club members or non-club-members, etc.

Many actors love to see what the competition is, but some will occasionally criticize this method, but only if they have never been on the side of the creative staff. For us, there are many advantages.

It is very hard to see how the cast looks and interacts with each other in a vacuum, which is how you see them if you bring them in to audition one at a time.

A director/choreographer/musical director would be at such a disadvantage if they couldn't see—to keep the *Hello, Dolly!* example alive—how your potential Dolly reads with your potential Vandergelder(s) or how your Barnaby(s) play off your Cornelius(s).

Could you imagine teaching a separate dance combination to forty people?

When sculpting an ensemble, you want to see how people look together—either because you want them all similar or you want them all different—either way you need an OPEN callback.

There is always feedback and scuttlebutt (love that word) when casting is announced from the people who weren't cast, wondering how so-and-so got the role. If the auditions are open, then everyone sees their competition, and while they might not acknowledge another person's superiority for a particular role, often they can at least see why the director went in a certain direction.

Now on to the callback process: Those auditioning arrive at 7 P.M. Based on your sheets, you take attendance, calling off audition numbers or names. You have three things to accomplish: you need to sing them, dance them, and read them, and, of course, you have to learn the material.

The best bet is to take the first hour or so to teach the material. If you have multiple rooms available to you, so much the better. While the choreographer is teaching the ensemble the dance combination, the rehearsal pianist or musical director might be teaching the principals some music. The stage manager can also hand out the scenes you are going to read for everyone to look over in between.

Once the ensemble is taught they can go off to another room to practice, or perhaps they now rotate to a music room to learn a song while the principals and support learn a different dance combination.

I tend to lurk around while the learning process is going on, getting yet another chance to observe the people I don't know.

Once everything is taught, it is generally best to get the dance out of the way, as this makes most of the nondancers very anxiety ridden.

We will have them do it en masse one more time with the rehearsal pianist then break them down into smaller groups of four or five.

Let's say you have a big enough space to do five at a time. You ask them to form two rows, with the downstage row in the "windows" of the upstage row.

	#1		#3		#5
		#2		#4	

You ask them to do the combination and then to hold where they finish in order for you to take notes. You then ask them to switch positions, and by this you mean they change front to back, not side to side—which takes some repetition before they get it right.

↑   #2   #4 ↓
    #1   #3   #5

This way you get to see people in the front as well as in the back, which can make a difference.

Ask them to stay still after this second time around for more notes, then bring on the next batch.

Next, you might move on to the vocals. One at a time each auditioner will sing what he or she learned. If time allows, I usually ask for two passes on the vocal audition, one purely for sound quality and to see if they have the notes, the second to imbue the audition with an interpretation of the piece.

The last step would be the readings, where you can mix and match performers to see who looks good with whom. You can explain the scene beforehand or just let the actors interpret, as they will. Again, if time allows, I might ask for a different interpretation—one that might never be performed that way in an actual performance but would show some variation.

Sometimes it even helps to line everyone up and just study them for a few moments, trying to get a sense of how people will look together.

Last, before everyone is dismissed, I'll mention the following: when rehearsals begin and a rough rehearsal schedule, suggesting that anyone who might have forgotten a conflict or two revisit their audition cards; when they will know our casting decisions, and whether everyone will be called regardless of a "yes" or a "no," or if only those who make it will be called, which is determined by the amount of people; and a thank you to everyone for putting up with what we know is a grueling and exhausting experience.

When three or four shows or musicals are cast at one time, it takes an awful lot of juggling to fill all roles properly, especially when some people might be good for more than one show. If you are casting only one show at a time, you have the luxury of going with your first choices. But I have found that even though someone attends the open call and all the callbacks, when the phone call is made to award them the role, they still turn it down. They might have auditioned elsewhere and wanted to see which theater offered them the juiciest role, and perhaps they realized they couldn't devote the time. Whatever the reason, it is best to have second and even third choices in case your first choices decline.

With the cast finally in place, rehearsals can begin.

The Rehearsal Process

I have rehearsed Equity shows where the entire process was completed in 10 days, working almost a 9 to 5 type of schedule. But in community theater, the great majority of your actors work other jobs 9 to 5, and so your rehearsal period is limited to weekends and evenings, often stretching out to four, six, or even eight weeks in length.

I tend to rehearse Monday through Thursday evenings from 7:30 P.M. until 10:30 P.M., and Sundays, from 1 P.M. until 7 P.M., which is like a double session.

This rehearsal period lasts six weeks, and a simplified breakdown for a musical might be as follows.

Six-Week Rehearsal Breakdown

Week 1:

Monday through Thursday P.M.—learn all music with musical director.

Monday/Tuesday: Principals work

Wednesday: Ensemble works

Thursday: All

Sunday: Entire cast—read- and sing-through

The cast sits around and reads through the script, singing as best they can when a musical number occurs. If there is time after a break, the choreographer might begin a dance number.

Week 2: Choreography and Blocking
With amateur dancers it is often helpful to get large musical numbers done right away, giving them all the time needed for brush-ups and cleaning. But it is good to vary the schedule, as they can go into overload very quickly.

Monday: Ensemble choreography

Tuesday: Principals, Act I, Scene 1, Scene 2

Wednesday: Ensemble choreography

Thursday: All, Act I, Scene 3

Sunday: Review musical numbers, block Act I, Scene 4

An overall review of everything wouldn't hurt as well.

Week 3: Very similar to Week 2, only hopefully you are moving on to Act II.

Week 4: By the end of Week 4 everything should be blocked and all numbers finished, and you should have been able to do what we call a "stumble-through" of each act, maybe Act I on Wednesday night and Act II on Thursday. A stumble-through is a cutesy term meaning running the act from top to bottom for the first time, hoping everyone remembers everything and gets to see the continuity after weeks of working just scenes and numbers.

They can be alternately hysterical and frustrating, and you need to approach them with patience and a positive outlook. It gets better from here—it has to.

Week 5: Primarily consists of run-throughs and cleaning sessions. During cleanings the choreographer will dissect each number, problem solving and drilling until it is as good as it gets.

Amateur performers often forget everything they learned from the musical director once they start to dance, so this is also a time to revisit all vocal lines, cut-offs, and harmonies.

This is also a good time for the various designers (lighting, set, costumes) to attend a run-through or two and work with the director on lighting cues, traffic patterns for set movements, and fittings for costumes.

Week 6: TECH WEEK (ahhhhh!!!) This is where it all comes together, where tempers can flare, and all are deprived of sleep.

Shows at Plays-in-the-Park open on Wednesday, so we have the luxury of about ten nights of tech. Other theaters might open on a Thursday or a Friday, which might result in less tech time, although if you are not an outdoor theater as we are, you might be able to start tech in the late afternoon. We have to wait until sundown.

I'll base my fictitious tech schedule on a seven-day tech week.

Tech Week

Day 1 and Day 2: If you have been rehearsing in a space other than the actual theater, this first tech rehearsal would be a restaging to the new space. Even if you have had the luxury of rehearsing on the performance space, most likely this would be the first rehearsal on the actual set(s) or at least portions of them. In either instance, this restaging takes time, and often we won't get further than Act I on the first day, in which case we pick it up with Act II on the next day, when more of the set will be in place.

The set designer and TD are on hand to help with the sets, and the stage manager works closely with them in getting them to function properly.

The lighting designer has been watching, seeing if the cues he or she had penciled in will work and adding and subtracting others.

Although many directors and choreographers give notes after every rehearsal, as opposed to fixing things as they occur, this is the time when you will certainly give notes after each rehearsal.

The giving, and taking, of notes is an art and a science all unto itself. Here's an ideal scenario:

You have an assistant who knows you well enough to understand what you mean when you speak very quickly and incoherently, which is most often the case when you are trying to watch something and communicate notes to your assistant at the same time. He or she can finish your sentences and knows exactly what you are referring to when you say something obtuse like "arms too high" during a dance number.

You are at a well-lit production table, with a laptop computer by your side and with an assistant who knows how to use Microsoft Word and Excel like a pro.

Then, with the cast assembled after the rehearsal on the stage, completely attentive to you and with pen and paper in hand, they listen to each and every note you give, whether it pertains directly to them or not, and they say "thank you" as they write down each personal note.

Yeah, that'll happen.

More than likely you are scribbling notes by yourself on a scrap of paper or on the back of a receipt, in the dark, writing illegibly.

When the time comes to give the notes, you have no idea what "arms too high" means, neither does the cast or your assistant, and you skip that note hoping it'll come back to you later. The cast doesn't have anything to write the notes down with, and they argue or defend each and every note you give. Half of them aren't listening; they're discussing last night's episode of *Will and Grace* and laughing hysterically.

Reality is something between those two extremes, and I make it a point to sit the cast down before the very first rehearsal, explaining the following important points:

- Everyone should listen to all the notes. Something directed at one person can ring true to others as well.

- Don't argue or defend a negative or constructive note. The time spent in discussion is unfair to the rest of the cast members, plus the note itself is often lost in all the discussion.

- Write the notes down. There is no way one can recall every note given to them, especially if they are in a leading role. It is best to write them down, then add them to your script and review them at some quiet time.

An alternative to sitting the cast down for notes is to go home and write all your notes down and either hand them out to the cast the next day or email them. I have done this as well and it has the advantage of stopping discussions, but it has the disadvantage of your not being able to imbue your notes with a passionate delivery.

As a producer, the one circumstance in which I do type my notes and hand them out is when I take the technical notes to the prop, set, costume, lighting, and sound people. By writing it out they have a checklist to work off of and they can all see what the other departments are doing.

Day 3: A full run-through, with set shifts happening (clumsily, most likely, but they will get smoother) and with as many of the props being used as possible. Generally, there are one or more propsters on board during tech and the run to set props and wait in the wings for hand-offs—if you've forgotten, that refers to handing props to the actor or taking props from the actor after the scene. Often you must stop each time an important prop is used to set the cue and assign personnel, and this is also a time when you find out what props are missing, or don't work, or aren't right.

The lighting designer might be sitting at the lighting board, putting "looks" up on stage (a "look" is a specific number of lights turned on in a specific cue, creating, say, a nighttime look, or a sunset) to check focus and effect, gearing up for tomorrow's cue-to-cue.

Day 4: Cue-to-cue. A cue-to-cue is exactly what it says—you go from one cue to the next, stopping to make whatever changes you need to. Cue-to-cue rehearsals generally are structured for the lighting designer but could also involve set changes, quick costume changes, pyrotechnics (called *pyro* for short—which generally must be executed by someone with a pyrotechnics license), and other special effects such as smoke machines, hazers, and strobe lights.

In other words, cue-to-cue rehearsals are for the technicians, with the actors just walking through their scenes. It is often tough on them (the actors) because the best way to do a cue-to-cue is to speed through or skip entirely scenes or passages where there aren't any lighting cues or props or set shifts.

The lighting designer, or if he is lucky enough to have an assistant who will run the board, sits at the console with his "cheat sheet" in front of him. A cheat sheet gives the channel numbers for the "looks" he has designed. It enables him to quickly bring up (illuminate) areas, or effects.

Channels and dimmers can get confusing, especially since everything involving the lights have numbers assigned to them.

The lighting instruments have numbers. They are plugged into circuits on the raceways, which have numbers. Cables run to dimmers, which have numbers. And the dimmers are assigned to channels on the board. More numbers.

Channel 23, for example, might bring up instruments 12 and 16, which are two-fered into circuit 112 and patched into dimmer 36. It can get confusing, but once you start to work with lighting it makes sense.

The LD will start to write cues, determining which lights come on, how bright or dim they will be (intensity), and how long it will take to come up or down (fade time) each time someone presses the "go" button on the lighting board.

The first cue is generally a preset cue—with the house lights up and either curtain warmers on if the front curtain is closed or a preset look illuminating the set in some interesting or pretty way.

Cue 2 is usually "house to half"—signaling the start of the show. Then house out (cue 3), followed by preset out (cue 4). Then he will build cue 5, which is the first look of the show.

Once completed, the LD will then tell the director that his or her first look is set, and the director will ask the actors to jump to the next place in the script where something technical happens. Maybe it's when a character enters the room and turns on a light switch, taking the room from the dim blue of cue 5 to a brightly lit space—and if this happens to be six pages into the script, the actors must quickly rearrange themselves to where they would be had they played the scene out up to this point.

The reason you need the actors on stage instead of just doing the cue-to-cue on an empty stage (which some theaters do indeed do—this is called a "dry tech") is that it is important to see how the lighting plays on humans. They might have been blocked far left or right, or far down or upstage, and until you actually see how the lights play on them, you won't know if your focus is correct. Additionally, if you are also cueing props and set moves, you certainly need the actors who handle them.

The process of writing a cue, then moving ahead to the next one, continues until you get to the final fade-out and house lights come up—a process that can take one or two or even more evenings depending upon the show and the complexity of the lighting and special effects. I remember clearly how long it took to cue *The Who's Tommy*, what with exploding pinball machines, rock show style lighting and incorporating video and slides.

Day 5: Might be a continuation of the cue-to-cue, or if you were lucky enough to get it all done the night before, you can start a run-through. Regardless, it is probably time to add in costumes to the mix.

One route some theaters take is to have a "costume parade" prior to rehearsal. A costume parade consists of having all the actors stand along the front of the stage (if applicable to your theater's configuration) and sort of model each costume, for the director's approval and for the costume designer to make notes.

While I suppose this could serve some purpose, unless you have an abundance of time, I prefer to just have the actors wear their costumes in the context of the run-through.

This way you get to see the costumes against the scenery, in the right lighting, and you also get to see if changes can be made on time, or if dressers would be needed in the wings to help the performers.

A costume parade works best if you have them the week before—it would then give the designers an idea of where things are going—but you rarely have the costumes ready a week before.

Day 6: It's time to start to deal with the orchestra. Because more often than not you have to pay the musicians, you most likely will only have one or two rehearsals with them. I have worked at community theaters where the musicians were volunteers along with the actors, but my memory of that experience is that it was a mixed bag—amateur musicians tend to have a tough time with Broadway scores. If your orchestra consists mainly of a rhythm section—piano, bass, and drums, maybe a guitar—then you can sometimes find hobbyists who are proficient on the bass and drums. But if you have any woodwinds, brass, or strings, you'll most likely need to turn to the pros.

On Day 6 you might begin your rehearsals earlier, starting off with a two- or two-and-a-half-hour orchestra rehearsal. This rehearsal is primarily for the conductor (who is often the musical director) as it is his time to let the musicians know all the cuts, possible rhythm shifts and any other changes particular to your show, and to make sure each musician knows what instruments they are doubling on. Doubling refers to when a single musician supplies and plays more than just one instrument. A Union musician would be paid extra for that.

Reed players typically double. The REED ONE book for *Hello, Dolly!* calls for the musician to play "Flute, Piccolo, Clarinet and Alto Saxophone." The flute would be his primary instrument; he would then be said to have three doubles, meaning he is also required to occasionally play three other instruments. Boy, he better be talented.

A gray area is percussion—the musician might have his trap set as his primary instrument (snare drum, bass drum, tom tom, high hat, and crash cymbal), but is also called upon to play tympani, mallet instruments (xylophone, orchestra bells, vibes), a cow bell, a ratchet, etc., etc. Hard to tell where doubles begin. Often the musician playing the trap set is the drummer, while the musician playing everything else is the percussionist.

Back to the orchestra rehearsal. I also find it helpful for the actors to sing along and for the dancers to mark the choreography. They have been rehearsing to a reduced piano score for the past few weeks, and suddenly there are accents and sounds that they never heard before. This often affects the choreography, and so as long as the musical director can do his thing without distraction, everyone can benefit from this first orchestra rehearsal.

After this rehearsal, and a short break for the MD, another run-through might be scheduled with the piano, or it might be a good night to take a break.

Day 7: This is the final dress rehearsal. For all intents and purposes it is run as a performance. It should start at the same time as performances, the full orchestra is present, and all costumes, props, lights, sound, and sets are in place.

With respect to an audience, I have mixed feelings. On the one hand, having a small audience of well-wishers attend the rehearsal does give the actors and staff an idea of where laughter and applause might occur. This could alter timing slightly, and you can judge from the audience's attentiveness (or lack of) if your ideas are being received and perceived. But dress rehearsals are notorious for mishaps, and even if nothing disastrous happens, pacing and energy are bound to be off as this is the first time with the orchestra and without starting and stopping. No matter how savvy your audience pretends to be, they are not seeing the show as you intend it, and I have often heard comments such as "Well, it'll get better." Their guarded word-of-mouth can prove detrimental. Try it for a few performances and form your own decisions. But make sure the people you do invite return later in the run, this time buying a ticket!

We have all heard the old adage, "Bad dress rehearsal, great opening" and like all old adages, it's true about half the time. But if you look at your dress rehearsal as one final chance to tinker, tweak, and fix, then regardless of how it comes off, it will have served its purpose—a final run-through that imitates an actual performance.

Did I say your dress rehearsal was one last chance to tweak? Shame on me.

I am a firm believer that in community theater the show is not "frozen" on opening night (meaning, you can no longer change things). In fact, I pride myself in some of the tweaks that my partner Michelle and I have made once the show is running. Sitting out in the audience during an actual performance provides a very different perspective of the work. You will see things you missed for the past six weeks. Story elements you assumed were clear suddenly aren't. Audiences may laugh in an unintentional spot, or you might realize that the timing is off here and there. Or you just might come up with new ideas. I clearly remember adding a very effective bit of business that I didn't think of until the closing night of *Sweeney Todd.*

Obviously making a radical change isn't fair, but refinements are perfectly acceptable. I make it clear to the cast that notes will be given right up until closing.

If you are directing a nonmusical, you might not need the full six weeks of rehearsal and might be able to do with a shorter technical schedule. But the basic steps involved work for whatever type of show you are doing. When you eliminate the musical director and choreographer from the mix, you remove a lot of necessary rehearsals, but the technical aspects still hold true.

Technical Aspects

There are a great many books detailing the technical and artistic aspects of lighting, costuming, sound, and set design and construction. Heinemann, who publishes this book, has a catalog full of wonderful books—even on choreography—so this chapter is merely to provide an overview of how these disciplines apply to the community theater and also to offer my own personal reflections.

When I suggest a product or service, it is because I have used it and like it, and it is not necessarily the recommendation of the publishers. I also don't mean to slight any company whose equipment or services I have never tried. I'm sure their products are great as well.

Set Design

Interestingly enough, most audience members are not really aware of the technical aspects of the show, unless those aspects appear truly tacky. They seem to be most aware of the set, because they look at it all night long, and then of the costumes, because clothing is something that applies to their daily lives. The average audience member rarely experiences the lighting on any level other than whether they can see clearly or not—which is a shame since lighting is perhaps the most artistic of all the disciplines.

I offer this lament not to be discouraging but rather to encourage you to keep striving to educate your audience to all aspects of the theatrical experience.

Let me preface my discussion on sets by making a statement that holds true for sets but really can be a mantra for all of community theater: what separates the professionals from the amateurs is the attention to detail. I mean this sincerely.

I have seen shows where the talent is good and the direction is fine but the show is diminished because of inferior production values, lacking in any detail. To make your sets out of corrugated cardboard is one thing—if that's all that's available to you, so be it—but to just throw a coat of paint on it and not to "dress it" at all is unforgivable.

To "dress a set"—which falls to the prop and paint department as well as the carpenters—means to add the details that make it a real, believable environment. But I'm jumping ahead of myself— we haven't built the set yet.

Obviously you'll need space to create it and tools with which to work. Having access to some sort of woodworking shop—either in a school or in town—would be a tremendous help. If you have space at your theater, even better, as you can build right on location and not have to truck scenery about.

And, of course, you need some people who know how to use the tools without losing a thumb. You usually can find some handymen (or handywomen) who love to do this sort of thing in their spare time, or maybe there is even a professional carpenter among the ranks who can guide other volunteers.

Safety first, of course—only let those who are experienced and knowledgeable handle power tools.

You will also wish to invest in some means to get high up when building or painting scenery. A good "A" frame ladder is essential; if you get one with a center extension, even better. The best one has a variable height from sixteen feet to thirty feet.

The next step up and a little more expensive would be to purchase some scaffolding. This allows you more access to your work, and it can be taken down and stored easily.

If you have a big theater, and money to burn, try securing a Genie lift. This is a battery or electrically powered device with an enclosed platform that can rise up quite high, sort of like a personal version of the buckets the phone company uses to reach the top of the poles.

The basic unit of most sets is the "flat." "Flats" are generally a stock item, and if you make them well they will last for a number of productions.

Flats are a wooden frame on which is either stretched muslin or luan. Luan is a relatively inexpensive sheet of wood, usually in a four foot by eight foot by one-eighth inch or one-quarter inch or one-half inch format. Luan holds up better, won't rip like muslin, and whereas it needs a base coat of white paint, it does not have to be "sized" like muslin. "Sizing" is a base coat applied to the muslin to shrink it a tad, pulling it taut on the wooden frame.

In addition to the choice of covering, the wooden frame can be made in two styles—Broadway flats and Hollywood flats. Broadway flats have the stiles, rails, and toggle blocks running flat against the covering, Hollywood flats have the stiles and rails running on edge, for added stability. This also provides a surface to screw or bolt them together.

The illustrations show the two types of flats, with their parts labeled.

If you are making stock flats, you'll want to make them the right height. If your battens trim at say fifteen feet off the deck, you'll most likely want your flats to be twelve feet tall, which you would make out of one and a half four-foot by eight-foot sheets of luan, which would let you get two flats out of every three sheets.

The flats can then be supported by angle braces and lashed together with rope and cleats on the back. You hide the seams with Dutchman—strips of fabric or paper glued on.

Angle braces can then support both types of flats. Broadways can be lashed together with rope and cleats on the back. Hollywoods can just be screwed together. You hide the seams with Dutchman—strips of fabric or paper glued on over the seams.

You can make flats with doors (you can fit a prehung door into a flat quite easily) and windows (either real ones or ones you've created), and if you design your sets carefully, you can mix and match them in a wide variety of configurations.

Flats make up the walls, doorways, and windows of almost any straight play that takes place in some sort of interior space—from the hotel rooms of *Lend Me a Tenor* to the barn of *Deathtrap* to the living room of *Arsenic and Old Lace*.

Flats can, of course, be exteriors as well if you need to see the buildings, such as the two backyards in *Mornings At Seven* or even the mansion in the musical *A Little Night Music*.

An example of a Broadway-style flat
Illustration by Jennifer Adamowsky, Related Media

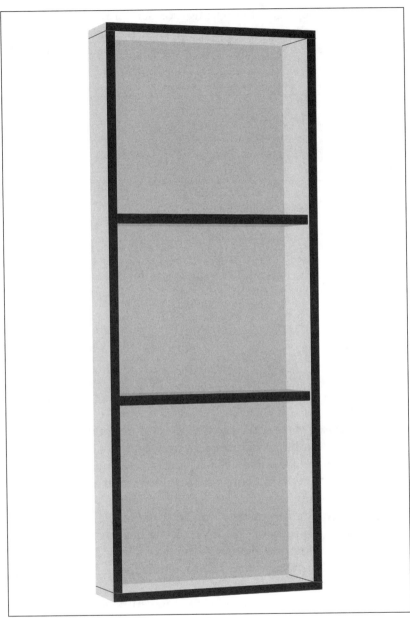

An example of a Hollywood-style flat
Illustration by Jennifer Adamowsky, Related Media

But what separates the boring "box set" of three simple walls from an applause-getting masterpiece is in the details.

Let's take a simple interior room. Instead of making the walls look like this:

Why not go for variety like this:

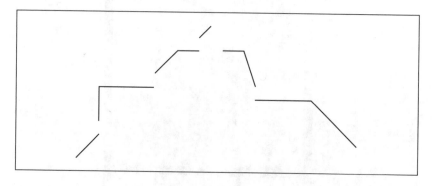

Add a staircase. Make a sunken living room by adding platforms upstage. Create a bay window or French doors, or a landing.

And then add details. Even if you make it out of Styrofoam (a very viable medium) you should always add floor molding, chair rail molding, and ornate ceiling molding (or whatever is called for). Try adding wainscoting to some of the walls.

Build a built-in bookcase. Show some heating pipes if appropriate. PVC tubing and elbows painted correctly look wonderful and very realistic. Make or find an old radiator and attach the pipes to it.

Then, when the structure is up, you can have a ball dressing the set. Try wallpaper, and if you are doing a set in disrepair, let some of it peel down. Add electrical outlets and light switches. Use ceiling lamps and floor lamps and make them practical (able to work on stage). Get working doorknobs and key plates. Put locks and peep holes on the front door.

In other words, create a reality. Whatever type of set you are designing, find the equivalent in real life, study it, and recreate those details.

I have set up a modest website with a few photos of sets I have designed, showing in many instances both the models and the actual finished product. There are also a few floor plans and elevations. If you have access to the Internet and are curious, type in the following link and take a peek at the details: *www.playsinthepark.com/scenicdesign/index.html*.

Musicals present a very different challenge to the community theater in terms of set design. With very few exceptions, musicals tend to have various locales and therefore have a lot of moving sets to contend with. (*The Fantasticks, Man of La Mancha*, and *You're A Good Man, Charlie Brown* are three one-set exceptions that come to mind.)

Therefore, one of the key elements in musicals are "wagons," which are actually platforms with swivel casters fastened to the bottom. These movable platforms hold all kinds of scenery and can be moved on and off by the stage crew dressed in black, or even by the actors as part of the show. When you see the scenery coming on and off, it is called "au vista." I have used wagons for everything from Gypsy's dressing room in *Gypsy* to the statue in the park in *The Music Man* to the Save-a-Soul Mission in *Guys and Dolls*.

The wagons can be made of four by eight by three-quarter-inch plywood, and two or more can be bolted together if you need a larger size. Use hefty casters that can hold a good deal of weight. And buy some "Rosco wagon brakes" to hold the wagons in place once they are rolled on to the stage.

Another staple of the musical is the painted drop or traveler. They are really the same type of item—a large piece of muslin, sewn together, and painted to represent something—but what defines the two types are how they are used. In the theater that has fly space, the drop would be attached to a pipe or batten. The drop would then be flown in and out on that pipe or batten. There is another small pipe sewn into a hem on the bottom of the drop, which keeps it taut and wrinkle free due to its weight. This is the optimum way to go but out of reach for most community theaters.

Most community theaters rely on travelers. A traveler is tied to wheels called "carriers" which glide in the channel of a traveller track, which is attached to a batten, enabling the drop to be pulled

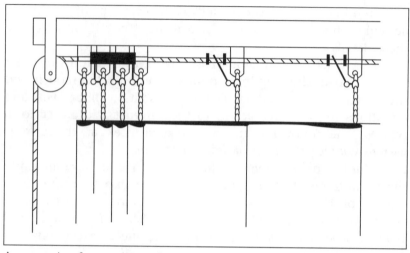

An example of a traveler track
Illustration by Jennifer Adamowsky, Related Media

on stage and off stage, similar to a shower curtain. This has several disadvantages—the drop has to be stored, all bunched up, either stage left or stage right, taking up space. It has a chain sewn into its bottom hem or pocket to keep it from blowing about, but that makes it noisy. And it can easily get caught and torn by lighting equipment or other scenery.

Still, if you "ain't got no flies," using a traveler is your only choice.

Flats and drops are referred to as two-dimensional scenery. They are for all intents and purposes, flat. Molding, real doors and windows, bookcases, plastic or Styrofoam brickwork, and the like, give a three-dimensional feel to flats. Staircases, which can roll on casters for musicals or be fastened down in a one-set show, are a great example of three-dimensional scenery. But free-form objects also go a long way to the realism—items such as trees, pillars, stumps, mounds, fountains, columns, etc., placed all over the stage, create realism.

Three-dimensional scenery gives much more reality to the overall design. Lighting illuminates three-dimensional scenery much more effectively, accentuating shadow and light. Two-dimensional scenery is good for backdrops, but it is merely the backdrop to which three-dimensional items are added.

Don't forget that instead of painting bricks, shingles, or stonework, making them dimensional is so much more effective. The aforementioned Styrofoam can be used to make terribly realistic yet lightweight bricks or stonework for exteriors. Order styro in four-foot by eight-foot sheets, about three-quarters of an inch thick, and carve away.

In fact, the more creative you get, the more you'll realize almost anything can be used in your set designs. Papier-mâché, fiberglass, steel, foam-core, chicken wire, and newspaper: all these craft items have found their way into one of my sets in one way or another.

Here's one of my favorite ways to add wonderful detail. If the audience sits close enough to the stage, using joint compound to give an old, textured look to almost anything works wonders. I have dabbed joint compound on everything from lampposts to doors and window frames to the bridge in *I'm Not Rappaport* and then stipple-painted it to give a very realistic weathered and textured look.

"Vac-form scenery" elements—available through most theatrical supply companies—are a very effective way to add realistic and dimensional walls, columns, and pilasters. Made out of a type of lightweight and flame-retardant material, it comes in panels, four foot by twelve foot, and is available in two different thicknesses, .015 and .030 mil. You can staple it to existing flats or simply frame it out. (Create a wooden frame to staple it to, as if you were making a luan or muslin flat.) It can be finished with theater paint. You can get the following types of panels: plain brick, old brick, cinder blocks, large and small fieldstone, bold stone, glass blocks, tiles, Spanish tile and cedar shingles (for roofs), clapboard, corrugated aluminum, and logs. Items such as fire hydrants, doors, and windows are also available.

Get yourself a catalog from Rose Brand (800-360-5056) or Norcostco (*www.norcostco.com*), or any of the myriad of theatrical houses, and study all the hardware and scenic construction items that are available for your use in your designs and sets.

I need to interject a word about "ground rows," and since this has several meanings and applications, this is as good a place as any. A "ground row" can refer to either a scenic element or a lighting element, and both are valuable tools. If you want to light a cyc evenly, you not only hang strip lights above and in front of the cyc but also place a row of strip lights on the stage deck

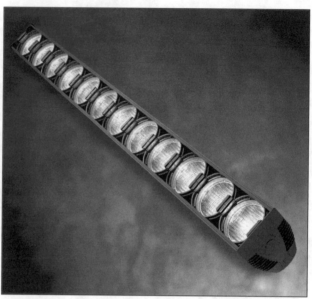

An example of a strip light, made by ETC
Provided by Patricia Bornhofen for ETC

pointing up at the cyc. By lighting the cyc from both the top and the bottom, you can get a very even distribution of color. By varying the color of the top strip lights and the bottom strip lights, you can create great effects such as a sunset or sunrise.

But there is a small problem: your audience will be able to see the row of strip lights on the floor. That's where the second type of ground row comes into play. Here you construct a scenic element to mask the lighting instruments. It can be something as simple as wooden strips about two or three feet tall, fastened to a base and painted black, that runs the length of the stage. This black ground row is less obtrusive than the lighting instruments.

Better yet would be to give this ground row some sort of silhouette. Maybe you cut the wood to resemble bushes and paint it in greens and browns. Perhaps you cut the wood to appear to be rocks. Whatever is appropriate to the show and the backdrop you are lighting.

But my favorite style of ground row is when you create one on a much grander size. For a production of *Oliver!* the set designer placed a cyc along the back wall of the theater. The lighting designer hung strip lights above and in front of the cyc and placed more below and in front of the cyc. The set designer then created an entire cityscape of London that stood almost twelve feet high, done in a forced perspective, meaning that the buildings left and right appeared closer and the buildings center were smaller and painted to appear to recede into the distance.

The lights on the stage deck not only lit the cyc but also appeared to give a glow above the tops of the "ground row" buildings. This technique can be used for a great many musicals and straight plays to create a "locale"—a cutout of River City for *The Music Man*, as a New York cityscape for *Guys and Dolls* or *Hello, Dolly!*, or in a whimsical way, giant comic strips for *You're a Good Man, Charlie Brown*. It's another alternative to a painted backdrop—and has the added benefit of a colorful cyc behind it, with all the lighting possibilities that it provides.

As a matter of fact, the illustration used to show an example of "how to grid" scenery (in the section on scenic painting) is actually of this ground row from *Oliver!*

Costumes

Costumes require research, no way around it. You will want to be true to the period and locale of your show, and the only way to do that is to study the period. There are many books that trace clothing through the ages, and of course if Hollywood has made a movie of the play you are working on (or something similar), that will come in very handy.

Once you have discovered the types of men's and women's clothing true to the period, there are three basic methods of obtaining costumes. I mentioned this earlier on—here is some more detailed information.

First would be to rent the costumes. There are a great many wonderful costume rental houses all across the country. If you are fortunate enough to be near one of them, the best bet is to have your designer actually go to the warehouse and choose the costumes. If not, you will have to rely on the company to pull your show for you. Before you sign anything or pay any money, ask to see photos of at least a few of the items, either via email or snail-mail. I list a few of the companies I am familiar with at the end of the book, but there are many more.

If you can't hand pick the costumes, the procedure usually is to ask the company to send you their costume breakdown sheet. Any reputable company will have one. This is either a series of sketches of the costumes or merely a list, broken down by each character and each scene.

It might look something like this:

CABARET
ACT I, SCENE 1—KIT KAT CLUB
Emcee: Period tails with glitter trim and vest
Cabaret girls: assorted short chorus costumes in poor taste
Girl orchestra: short dresses and hats, very tacky
Waiters and busboys: uniforms according to station
Entertainers: variety of European Music Hall costumes, i.e., Ventriloquist, Magician, etc.

The list will go on for each scene and each character.

Study the list carefully. You may decide that you don't need every costume listed—that you can secure some of them elsewhere. Sometimes theaters rent the costumes for the principals, which usually are the grandest, and find the ensemble costumes elsewhere. In general, men's period suits are very hard to come by and often merit renting. It would be criminal to put the inhabitants of *Titanic* in polyester leisure suits from the 1970s.

You then fill out the measurement forms that the company will send you for everyone who is to wear a rented costume, determining:

Name of actress

Character

Height

Weight

Head/hat size

Neck size

Sleeve size

Bust size (if applicable)

Waist size

Hip size

Waist to floor measurement

Neck to waist measurement

Shoulder to shoulder measurement

. . . and often many other dimensions. The more information you give them, the better they can initially pick the costume and then do the alterations.

Costumes can be anywhere from $60 to $150 each for the first week, then half that for each subsequent week, plus all the shipping and often dry cleaning. Often the price goes down the more items you rent. If you are close enough to the rental house to hand pick the costumes, you can work different deals. We will often do the alterations ourselves in exchange for not having to have the costumes cleaned.

Once you find a costume house you like, stick with them. They'll reward you with great costumes and great value and sometimes will even build special costumes for you, which then become part of their stock.

If you are looking for the original Broadway designs, which many houses stock, make sure you request just that. Otherwise, they may pull from the period without being specific to your show. If you want the Broadway design for the closing of *A Chorus Line* you'll need to request it; or if you are looking for Dolly's red dress you need to specify, as often these much-requested items are already out on rental.

If you can afford it, renting costumes is a very good and reasonably easy way to make your production look professional. Consider renting whenever you do a show set in a time period other than "now" or in the recent past.

If you are doing a show from the 1950s on up, you might consider one of the other methods to obtain costumes . . . the second of which would be to buy and/or refurbish existing clothing.

Peter Allen once sang: "Everything old is new again." Right now if you were trying to costume *Hair* or *Sweet Charity* or *Kennedy's Children* you would very likely be able to find suitable costumes in your local mall or thrift stores. With a little ingenuity, costumes from the past few decades can usually be bought or found in closets and attics, and if you have a clever seamstress in your ranks, they can be refurbished and altered to give the proper flavor.

It pays to try and collect interesting clothing such as double-breasted and vested suits or wedding gowns or colorful day dresses. One such way to do so is to include a mention in your program that you happily accept donated clothing, in good condition, of a "period" look.

Obviously you need to be careful that you don't become a dropoff spot for anyone wishing to dispose of clothing that is too small or too big or too distressed for them to wear—that's the domain of Good Will and other organizations—and you certainly want to stay away from most anything made out of polyester (especially leisure suits!)—but you'd be surprised at the good stuff that will get dropped off at your doorstep.

I have found that as long as there is something usable in the "drop off," the nicest thing to do is to take it all, be profusely grateful, then take what you don't want to a Good Will dropoff yourself. You might also look into whether these donations are tax deductible for the donator, which would be another reason for them to donate.

As an aside, we often "advertise" in our program for all kinds of donations: computers and peripherals, suitcases and steamer trunks, old telephones, antiques of any sort, etc. If you have the storage, it's a great way to accumulate interesting props and set pieces.

Of all the ways to acquire costumes, perhaps the most difficult method is the third method: to design and build costumes from scratch.

This is usually best left to professionals, but occasionally you can latch on to a design student on their way up who will work at your theater for the experience and the exercise.

Designing and building costumes requires someone who is skilled enough to:

1. research and have the talent to envision a costume worth building
2. have the ability to draw the design for the director to approve it
3. know how to create the pattern for the stitchers to create the work
4. know how and where to shop for material and trim
5. know enough about draping, cutting, and sewing to actually bring the design to life

I have found that for most shows, this one-third rule seems to apply. We usually rent about a third of the costumes needed for a specific show—either hard to get items, easily recognizable items, items for hard-to-fit-people, or costumes for the principals.

Next, we find about one-third of the costumes from our stock or in stores and embellish and change them as needed. Last, we create about one-third of the costumes from scratch, which gives our designers a creative outlet and also adds new blood to our stock. If possible, try to have the designers make the costumes a tad large, allowing for alterations in the future.

Amass enough stock and you can start to rent them out yourself, which is time consuming but lucrative. Just make sure that you have a contract that states such things as: no alterations to be made without permission, costumes are to be dry-cleaned before returning, damages will be paid for, and costumes will be returned by the agreed-upon date.

Lighting

Now we're into a subject dear to my soul. You can do a show with almost no scenery. You can dress in black leotards. You can mime props. But good lighting is essential!

My love of lighting goes back to my days at Celebration Playhouse, where, because of the mere eight-foot ceiling, we had to light our shows with a collection of "inkies," an affectionate name for three-inch fresnel-lens spotlights ("fresnels"). Despite the fact we were using what some might consider "toy" lights, we managed to create stunning effects through the use of color medium, gobos, and a clever light plot.

Lighting has come a long, long way in terms of the equipment—intelligent computerized lighting instruments and control consoles (sometimes called lighting boards), tiny dimmer packs, all sorts of projections—and so it is possible to create virtually every mood with lights. In fact, you can even use lighting *instead* of scenery.

As with all the other technical disciplines, there are books out there that will teach you the mechanics and the theory of lighting. And as with the other disciplines, I'm here merely to give you pointers from my experience.

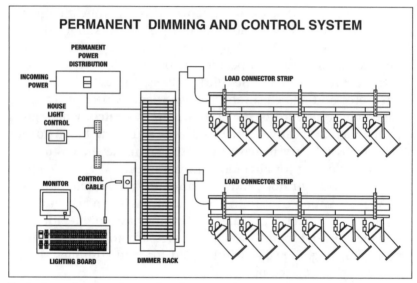

Illustration of a permanent dimming control system
From the Norcostco catalog

Make sure, in addition to a good lighting designer, you also utilize a good electrician. A great deal of amperage is needed to light a theater, and it can be dangerous. But let's assume you know that and have the personnel you need to light your shows.

First, let's talk equipment. In simplest terms, you take a lighting instrument, hang it up, run a cable from it to a dimmer pack, and plug it in. Then you plug a control console (or "board") into the dimmer pack and use a control to fade the light up and down. Not much different from what's in your dining room. Where it gets complicated is when you have a hundred lights, fifty dimmers, a mess of cable, and you need to control banks of lights at a time.

Take a look at the Permanent Dimming and Control System diagram as it appears in the Norcostco catalog.

Best let your lighting designer and master electrician handle all of that. And if you are just starting out, make sure you talk to the electric company so that you get the right amount of power into your building. Let the reps from the lighting equipment company come to the theater and work with you on the right dimmer packs, racks, and connections.

But it is helpful if you, as producer, know a bit about the lighting instruments themselves, so—the $2.00 tour. Here, from the Norcostco catalog is a brief Lighting Fixture Guide.

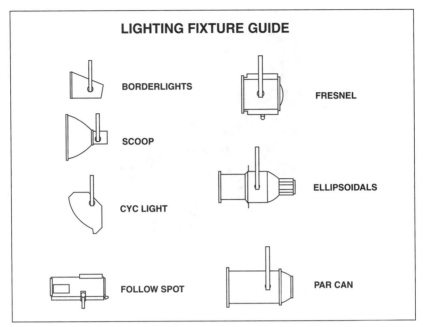

Lighting Fixture Guide
From the Norcostco catalog

Note that ellipsoidals are sometimes more commonly known as Lekos—which is actually a brand name, Lekolite by Strand. They have also been known as profile spots.

Now, an opinion: I have used all sorts of lighting instruments from all manufacturers, and I must say that I like the equipment made by ETC (Electronic Theatre Controls, Inc.) a lot. Their ellipsoidal, the Source Four™ is one of the most versatile and user-friendly instruments I have ever worked with.

Because of its design, you don't burn your fingers changing gels (although you should always wear gloves), and focusing and shutter-cutting is a joy. Theater terms often have more than one meaning. "Focusing a light" most often refers to aiming the instrument carefully in order to light up a specific area of the stage in a specific size, without having light bleed on to areas that are not meant to be illuminated. Shutter-cuts refers to the four devices on the sides of the instrument, between the lamp and lens, that move in and out; this allows the designer to create sharp lines out of the projected light beam.

ETC also makes wonderful computerized lighting control consoles. Take, for example, the Expression 3™. It has three

Photo of a Source Four™ Ellipsoidal by ETC
Provided by Patricia Bornhofen for ETC

universes (separate outputs) of DMX (see the end of the chapter), which means it can control moving lights, scrollers, and other lighting accessories without resorting to a separate board. It has ten pages of twenty-four submasters, so you would never run out of different looks in a community theater environment, and it holds hundreds of cues.

A "look" is a grouping of lights, controlled by a single submaster slider. By having so many submasters available, you can preprogram your lighting plot's looks, making the technical rehearsal that much easier.

This board is more than enough for any community theater.

I mentioned gels and gobos . . . what are those? *Indispensable* is what they are.

Gels are a color medium that come in sheets and rolls and are cut to fit the front of a lighting instrument. They fit into a "gel frame" and transform the beam of light into any one of hundreds of beautiful colors. They eventually burn out, and so are considered disposable, although glass ones (called dichroics) that last longer are available at a higher cost. The more saturated the color, the less light can pass through the gel, so you may have to use more instruments to get that indigo night sky you are hoping for.

Photo of an Expression 3™ Control Console by ETC
Provided by Patricia Bornhofen for ETC

ROSCO, GAM, APOLLO, and LEE all make gels and they will be happy to send you their swatch books, which, in addition to color medium, contain diffusion filters, which make the light softer.

Gobos—also called patterns and breakups—are thin metal discs that have a design or picture cut into them. These "patterns" sit in a holder between the lens and the lamp, an area of the instrument called the gate. They create images, such as branches, bricks, clouds, lightning, windows, or just patterns (hence the name breakups).

Again, ROSCO and GAM both make them, and will send out a catalog. You can also have them make custom gobos for you, created from logos or other artwork.

Armed with gels and gobos, lighting becomes art. Rather than using light to enhance the theatrical experience, too often a community theater is content to just make sure the performers can be seen.

What follows is a little lighting scenario I made up to exemplify how you might use light in a creative way. It is designed to show you how you can "do a lot with a little." We'll keep in mind some basic concepts: we need to light the actors from the front for visibility; from the back, side, and top for dimension; and we need to light the environment. We also need to concern ourselves with how the lights will be positioned and focused and with how the dimmers and the lighting board will control them. Last, we'll want to add gels for color and gobos for interest and effect.

Picture a black box theater space. The floor is black, and there is a white cyc against the back wall.

Our scene is "A Wooded Area at Night." That's what it says on page one of the script.

Our lighting inventory is somewhat limited, but we have twelve Fresnels, twelve ellipsoidal reflector spotlights, and six par cans (par 64). We have eighteen dimmers rated at 2,400 watts each, which can take two instruments each, using a 1,000-watt lamp (the pars and the ellipsoidals), or four instruments lamped with 500-watt lamps (the Fresnels). Note that there are the new HPL lamps, which are 575-watt lamps, but give out as much illumination as a 1,000-watt lamp. Most ETC instruments, and many others, accept these lamps.

We have four pipes to hang lights on—one is over the audience, called our FOH (front-of-house) position, and the first, second, and third electrics are over the stage. Here's one way to attack the challenge:

First we want to create a deep blue ambience. For that, it would be best to use the Par 64s, which can cover a wide area in strong light. We want to use three dimmers, so we will gang two instruments together using "two-fers," which is a length of cable with two female ends to plug lights into, and one male end, to plug into the dimmer, or into an extension cable that goes into the dimmer. We have lamped our instruments with 1,000-watt WIDE par lamps. (They come in medium, narrow, and very narrow as well, but we want coverage.)

Two of the pars will be on our front-of-house batten or pipe, focused on the playing area, two more will be on the second electric above the stage, pointing straight down, and the last two will be on the third electric, focused softly on the cyc.

We will use Roscolux gel #80—primary blue—as our color filter.

Next, we'll want to add some light to illuminate the actors. Here we'll use the Fresnels, lamped with 500-watt lamps, allowing us to gang four together, using two, two-fers each. We'll put four on the front of house batten focused downstage, four on the first electric focused upstage, and four on the third electric to be used as backlight. Backlight will serve to add dimension to the actors and separate them from the backdrop.

We will cross-focus the lights to create a nice look on faces—lighting from straight on is not very flattering.

All of the ellipsoidals reflector spotlights are set to flood position for greater coverage and overlap. For our choice of gels, we'll use Roscolux #60, which is called "No Color Blue."

We have used up six of our dimmers so far—three for the par cans and three for the Fresnels. We have twelve dimmers and twelve ellipsoidal reflector spotlights left.

Now comes the fun part. For our special effects, we are going to use our ellipsoidal reflector spotlights, which, if you remember, can be focused and shuttered. For maximum control, we are going to hook them up in what is referred to as a "one to one" hard patch—each ellipsoidal reflector spotlight is going to be plugged directly into its own dimmer.

In the best of all possible theatrical worlds, you will have enough dimmer for each of your instruments and can always do a "one to one" hard patch. Then you would group instruments together to come up at the same time electronically using the lighting board's memory—called a soft patch.

We want a moon on our backdrop, and since our play takes place over a week, we want it to change phases. We need to dedicate two ellipsoidal reflector spotlights to this task.

We will place them both on the first electric, one left and one right, and this time we will focus them straight on to the cyc to avoid key stoning, which is when the image bends a bit. This is very evident when you are watching slides of your vacation to Quebec and the slide projector is shooting up at the screen.

We are going to use gobos in our ellipsoidal reflector spotlights—this time by Gam—D250 "Crescent Moon" and D794 "Moon with Clouds." By moving the barrel of the lens in and out we can focus the image created by the gobo sharply, but if we want it even sharper, we use what is referred to as a "Donut"—which is a circle cut in a metal that is used to concentrate the light, therefore making it sharper.

Ellipsoidals come with various lens sizes, such as a six by four and a half, six by nine, six by twelve, six by sixteen. When you are using a gobo—in fact, anytime you use an Ellipsoidal—you want to choose the right one for the job.

The way to decide which instrument to use is to think of them in this light, so to speak.

Given the same distance from the instrument to the subject—say ten feet—the four and a half would cover the widest area, but at the expense of intensity. The six by sixteen would cover the least amount of subject matter but would shine the brightest. A little experimentation goes a long way to getting the most from your instruments.

Source Fours™, and other ellipsoidals such as the Shakespeare series by Altman, have interchangeable lenses, which makes things easier—you can leave the instruments where they are and merely swap out the lens barrels.

We won't use any gels for our moon—white light seems to do just fine.

As always—an aside. There is another effective way to make the Moon or the Sun, and that is with a "light box." You'll need room upstage of your cyc. You create a box out of plywood—say four feet by four feet by eight inches deep. The back is solid plywood, and the front is the cutout of a circle or a crescent. Along all four walls are placed porcelain lighting sockets, fitted with twenty-five-watt bulbs (maybe six to a side—twenty-four total). When this light box is placed up against the cyc and lit, you get a very effective image of the Moon or Sun (depending upon brightness) shining through. Vary the distance from the cyc to change the focus. This is also the way to do signage or stained glass windows or, well, anything you can imagine.

Back to our lighting project. We now have two different Moons, and we would fade up a different one for Act I, and the other for Act II.

Let's add "stars." Use three ellipsoidal reflector spotlights, each on the second electric, with the widest lenses you have.

We'll cross focus them a bit to cover the whole cyc and outfit them with realistic gobos, say GAM D337 Nebula. No gel— white light is good.

Okay, five of our twelve ellipsoidals used—seven more to go.

Remember we're in the woods, and a great effect is to see the actors moving in and out of the light of the moon shining through the branches of the trees. So we're going to dedicate five of our ellipsoidals to "branches." We'll put two of them on our FOH pipe, focused upstage, two will go on the third electric focused downstage, and one will go on the second electric focused straight down on the floor.

For gobos we'll use Rosco D7732 "Realistic Leaves" by Tony Walton in two units (one each on the third), Rosco D7735 "Bare Branches" by Robin Wagner in two units (one each on the FOH), and in our center unit, Rosco D7733 Dense Leaves by Ming Cho Lee (all famous Broadway designers).

For color, we're going to get tricky. We're going to combine two gels in each instrument by cutting them in half and holding them together with gaffer's tape, so we have a real mixture of colors: Roscolux #93 Blue Green and #16 Light Amber.

Now, how will we utilize our final two instruments? In our imaginary script, there is a moment at the end of Act I when the two main characters stand at opposite ends of the stage, and as the lights fade around them, they are left in two "specials" for their final dialogue.

A "special" is any light that illuminates a specific thing, such as an actor, a clock on a wall, a fireplace, whatever. Specials usually need their own dimmer as they are controlled separately, so always leave room for a few of these when planning your plot.

We'll hang our last two remaining ellipsoidals on the FOH pipe. We'll ask the stage manager or a techie standing by to stand exactly where the two actors will stand at the end of Act I. We'll take spike tape (never masking, gaffers, or duct tape—all will leave a sticky residue on the stage floor) and mark a small X in yellow so the actors can always hit their "mark," which is indicated by the "spike mark." We'll focus the lights in tight beams right on the stand-ins' faces. We'll throw the focus (sometimes referred to as "running the barrel") so that there are no hard edges, just soft light.

Let's get these instruments with Roscolux #33 "No Color Pink" to make our actors look nice 'n purty.

How could we improve upon this plot if we had more instruments and dimmers available? Glad you asked. Let's say we had a few more Fresnels. The first place I would embellish are the specials. To really create a beautiful effect at the end of Act I, it would be good to tie in a "down light" and a "back light" to our front light. The down light would hang directly above the actor and point straight down. The back light, hung on the pipe directly upstage of the actor's spot, would be focused on the back of their heads, which would produce a bit of a halo effect. This would give a much more effective image.

Next I would add side lighting. Side lighting, essential in dance shows or for dance numbers in musicals, is done with instruments (generally ellipsoidals, which can be shuttered and focused) mounted on vertical pipes screwed into boom bases and placed in the wings or, in our case, on the sides. You could also use "tail downs" which are pipes that hang down vertically from the battens and give you a very high side shot. You can also use light stands called booms just offstage behind the legs. The lights are placed at varying heights, from "shin busters" (known because dancers invariably crash into them as they "*chasse*" or "*bouree*" into the wings), which are about a foot off the ground, to mid-height (maybe three or four feet off the deck) to head height, and anywhere in between.

Side lighting also helps to define actors and shapes. In lighting, shadows are as important as light.

If striplights (also called X-ray, cyc lights, or border lights) were available, they would have a purpose in our plot as well. A striplight is generally used to light a cyc or a piece of scenery and has two, three, or four circuits so you can group colors together. They can be placed on a batten just down of the scenery, where it would light it from above, or on the deck, focused up at the scenery. Ideally, for a smooth even wash of color, you would do both.

If you are using a three-circuit series of strips and you gel them alternately blue, red, and amber, you could not only turn the cyc blue, red, or amber, but a zillion combinations of the three as well (okay, maybe not quite a zillion, but a whole lot).

We should now have a living environment that shouts "woods at night," even though there is no scenery.

Want to really make an impact? Rent or buy a "hazer" which throws particles of moisture into the air and allows you to actually see the shafts of light, just as you would in a misty forest. Hazers are staples at rock concerts and are beginning to be so at theaters as well. Can't do a show that takes place in London without one!

Add a sound effects track of hoot owls and cicadas and you'll be complete.

See the lighting plot in the following illustration for a rough, hand-drawn idea of how this plays out on paper.

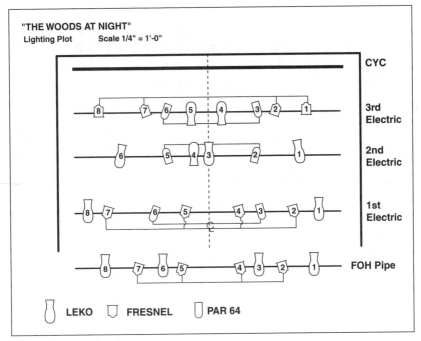

Example of a lighting plot
Designed by Gary Cohen; drawn by Jennifer Adamowsky, Related Media

Obviously my example was a simplistic one, but if you analyze each scene in your play and think in terms of front, back, side, and downlight, color, gobo, and kind of focus, you can support the play tremendously.

The use of "follow spots" can be very helpful in an overall lighting design, particularly in musicals, although they have their place in nonmusicals as well. Follow spots are lighting instruments with very long "throw" (the length the light can travel from the unit to the actors' faces) and very bright illumination. They are placed on stands, which enable them to be easily moved, and their focus can be changed from soft to a very crisp circle. They also hold several "gels" in a changer (also called a boomerang), so that their color can be changed.

The purpose of a follow spot is simply to produce a spot of light with more illumination than the surrounding area.

The most obvious use for a follow spot is to make the leading performer "stand out" or "pop" when singing a song in a musical.

This enables you to fade down all the other lights—perhaps create a dreamlike mood rather than a realistic one—and the performer will still be seen clearly. Obviously if you are illuminating a duet, a trio, or a quartet, it helps to have more than one follow spot. Professional theaters often have four or more, some of them located in the wings or on trusses behind the performers, allowing for moving side and backlights, which can be a spectacular effect.

The position of the spots is very important. Ideally, you let the area where the spot will "live" dictate the type of spotlight you will purchase, in terms of size, illumination or punch, and throw distance ability, but often you inherit a spotlight and then have to find a spot for it to live.

Another aside—referring to where something "lives" seems to be common in theaters and can be a fun word to toss around. It refers to the area on the set or in the theater where something is placed, often on a semipermanent basis, at least for the run of a show. You might say: "The ladder will live offstage right" or "The electric keyboard can live in the pit."

I have found there are two basic effects created by a follow spot, and their position is one factor in determining these looks. When a follow spot is placed head on with the performer and focused to a crisp circle, you get a very theatrical look that an audience perceives as something reminiscent of vaudeville, burlesque, or nightclubs.

This would not be my first choice for ninety percent of the musicals you might produce and certainly has little use in a straight play. A handful of applications come to mind—the spotlight on Gypsy Rose Lee during her strip in *Gypsy*, the spotlight that is referred to in song "Broadway Baby" from the musical *Follies*, the production numbers in *Funny Girl*—in other words, shows that are about show business, when you wish to recreate an old-fashioned look. *Cabaret* uses spotlights in this theatrical way, and even *The Producers*, a "new" musical, uses spotlights in a traditional manner.

The way a follow spot should be used for all the rest of the musicals is from a higher angle, say thirty degrees, with the beam of light from the follow spot set at a very soft focus. It might even be helpful to use a frost gel, also called a diffusion gel, to soften the edges of the light even further than the unit itself allows.

Using a follow spot with a soft focus beam, aimed from a high angle, the actor merely glows brighter than his surroundings, rather than giving the appearance of having a circle of light following him.

Handling a follow spot takes some practice. One of the most difficult aspects is finding your subject. A practiced operator can usually find his or her actor by focusing in the general vicinity and then glowing the light ever so slightly. As soon as the actor is centered in the light, the instrument's intensity can be increased.

The FS (follow spot) operator needs to know the movements of the performers assigned to his or her unit so that they can be followed in a smooth manner. It is best to have the "spot ops" watch the show once with a cue sheet in hand and then rehearse for at least two run-throughs. (Hint for spot ops—have the operators follow the actors' hips: this way they are not thrown off by the actor moving their head in a dance. If they stay centered on the hips, the actor will always be in the light.)

And now for something completely different—a word about "practicals." By theatrical definition, "practicals" are lights that can be seen as part of the set—chandeliers, desk and floor lamps, fireplaces, sconces, Rosco candles (a very realistic prop made by Rosco using a flicker lamp to simulate a candle), streetlamps, etc.

"Practicals" add detail to a set and breathe life into it. They often give you a "source" for your theatrical lighting—in other words, where the light on the set appears to be coming from. If you have a streetlamp stage left, you would support the light emanating from it with theatrical instruments. I guess the moon is one giant practical.

I'll leave this chapter with a word about "DMX"—which is a new type of standard control protocol between the lighting control board, dimmers, and instruments and accessories. Huh?

In simpler terms, DMX is a way that a computerized lighting board can "talk" to the dimmers and other high-tech lighting devices such as color scrollers, moving lights, hazers and fog machines, and other pieces of equipment. If you are starting your theater from scratch or refurbishing and can afford to go the DMX route, by all means it is recommended.

Props

As an actor, I always loved props. Give me a cane, or a drink to mix, or a cigar, and my character is made. I know in a lot of community theaters, props are merely a necessary evil—and they are often scrounged at the last minute. This is too bad, as props are terribly important. I group into this category "set dressing," which are "props" used by the set and not by the actor.

I go back to my mantra—what separates the amateur from the pro are the details. The creation of props should certainly support this statement.

Like costumes, props can be rented, bought, or built. In the New Jersey area we are lucky enough to have two splendid prop houses: PRISM in Rahway (1-888-40-PRISM) who often carry the props from defunct Broadway shows, and ANYTHING BUT COSTUMES in Flemington (609-397-3970). Both places have everything from hand props to furniture and oodles of goodies in between.

Check phonebooks or online to find similar goldmines in your area. When a difficult prop is needed—a chandelier, an antique sewing machine, Tevye's cart—try the rental houses first.

Next option, if budget permits, is to buy the item. Not to overstate the obvious, but props can be bought in almost every type of store—from dollar parlors, to silk flower stores, to arts and crafts stores, to the local grocery store.

There are also specialty houses for theatrical props available via catalog or over the Internet. A small sampling would be:

- Home Decorators (*www.homedecorators.com*): almost anything
- Flex Molding (Hackensack, NJ, 201-487-8080): plastic molding and simulated wood carvings for furniture
- Navy Arms (*www.NavyArmsMSD.com*): military surplus
- The Iron Shop (1-800-523-7427): spiral staircase kits
- Outwater Plastics (Woodridge, NJ): architectural items in plastic, such as fireplaces, columns, and millwork
- Tri-Ess Sciences, Inc. (213-245-7685): special effects, including skeletons
- Putnam Rolling Ladder Co. (212-226-5147): ladders and more
- Phoneco, Inc. (608-582-4124): replicas and working phones of every period

- Rick's Movie Graphics (800-252-0425): posters, etc.

- Costume Armour (914-534-9120): theatrical armour

- Tuxedo Wholesaler (800-828-2802): tuxes and uniforms

- LeMaitre (800-388-0617): pyro and special effects (safety first, remember)

This is, of course, a mere scratching of the surface, but it gives you an idea of what is out there—and enforces the fact that everything is indeed available if you look hard enough.

The third option for the "propster" would be to build what is needed, and here ingenuity reigns supreme. Time to get out your papier-mâché, your chicken wire, your corrugated cardboard, your string, and your hot glue gun.

The distance your audience sits from the stage will determine how much you can get away with. And so will the style of the show. If you were doing the set decorations and props for *American Buffalo* in a small theater, you would want to fill your junk store with real items. But if you were doing that old favorite, *Hello, Dolly!*, and during the "Waiters Galop" your dancers threw turkeys about and dueled with oversized shish kabobs, you might make everything out of Styrofoam—carved, covered, and painted.

Let taste and artistry be your guides. If you are filling a bookcase that is close to the audience, use real books. If the bookcase is upstage and in a stylized musical such as *My Fair Lady*, you might just get away with realistically painted luan, cut with the silhouette of various book sizes. Some designers prefer realistic set dressing; others might actually welcome the "cartoonish" look that two-dimensional painted items provide.

The computer is invaluable for the propster. It can be used for research—just about anything can be found on the Internet. Recently I needed to design a lectern, and by searching "lecterns" I found photos of close to seventy-five I could model mine on.

Another use for the computer is to couple it to a printer and actually use it to make props. I have printed out color photos of foreign currency, enlarged them to the actual size, printed them out, and used them as prop money. I have taken photographs of oil paintings or portraits, enlarged them, framed them, and used them as set decoration. With the myriad of fonts available on the Internet, signs of almost any design can be created. If you print lettering out onto sheets of clear plastic, you will have signage for a window made of Plexiglas or glass.

It is helpful to invest in a printer than can print on up to seventeen-inch by twenty-two-inch paper for use in the prop shop.

Some items to have on hand include glue guns and sticks of glue, Ethafoam rod stock (a pliable round core of Ethafoam which is sold by the foot and can be used to decorate furniture, picture frames, or even costumes), sheets of Styrofoam of various thickness, sheets of polyurethane foam in various thickness, rope, clothesline, newspapers, Kraft paper (a brown paper sold in rolls), sheets of Foam Core, sheets of matte board, rolls of foil, construction paper, stencils of lettering, numbers and even designs used for repeating wallpaper, glitter, "Rigid Wrap" for making casts (it is premixed—just wet it), "Friendly Plastic," "Goop"—a great glue, fabric glue, chicken wire, scraps of fabric, rubber cement, all kinds of wire, plastic and silk flowers and leaves/vines, etc.

All of the aforementioned items and scores of other household, craft, and hardware store products can be used in fashioning props. All it takes is imagination and a touch of artistry. Whatever you do, just keep the details in mind!

Special Effects

Special effects can fall under any of the previously cited production categories. They include, but are certainly not limited to, smoke machines and hazers, fire effects and explosions on stage, magic on stage, black lights and hydraulics. Let's also group slide shows and computer graphics in this category.

Let's take a look at some of these. I already mentioned hazers (and my love of them), and whereas they are sometimes used in conjunction with a smoke machine, they are not the same animal. Hazers put the cloud of mist in the area so that the beams of light and their color are visible. Smoke machines use various types of fog fluids, the most recent and best being water based, to create a dense fog/smoke that can be used for cloud effects, burning buildings, and horror scenes such as in *Dracula* or *Jekyll & Hyde*.

Smoke machines have their down sides, although I would never think twice about using them. If an overzealous techie controls them, they can easily pour out much more smoke than needed. They can set off fire alarms and sprinklers—and you should always warn the local fire department you are using one in your show. They usually need a fan to suck or blow the smoke off stage and direct them away from the audience.

There is a little documented side effect as well. Approximately ninety seconds after a fog machine sends out its first burst of smoke, you will note members of the audience starting to cough. Not because the smoke has reached them—in most cases it hasn't—it's just a Pavlov's dog reaction—smoke machine = coughing.

Pyrotechnics, or pyro, is often needed in a show, from a simple burst of a smoke pot (*Hello, Dolly!*), to a smoking mushroom (*Peter Pan*) to an exploding pinball machine (*The Who's Tommy*), to lit torches (*Oliver!, King and I*).

Safety first. Pyro can be dangerous. It bears repeating that the technician handling pyro needs to licensed or certified.

The best way to handle it is with professional equipment, and to that end I recommend products by Le'Maitre. They sell firing pods and controllers that I have found to be easy and safe to use if you follow their instructions. Then you buy something called a gerb if you want a fountain spray of sparks. Or try a Phantom Flame and Colored Smoke cartridge as well as Pyroflashes for mushroom cloud effects. If you use an array plate you can use several gerbs or pyroflashes for an even more dramatic effect.

Black lights are interesting to use on stage. There is a company called Wildfire who make both the Ultraviolet Fixtures and the Wildfire water-based acrylic paint in about fifteen or so colors. Rosco makes fluorescent paint as well.

One fun use for black light involves muslin drops. By double painting the drop—once using theater paint, then on top of it using fluorescent paint—you can get two uses out of the same drop. The best example would be to paint an exterior "day" scene on to a drop, say of Broadway marquees, and then paint the same scene again, this time with fluorescent paint, as if it were at night and all the bulbs were lit. During your "day scenes," when the drop is lit with regular theater lights, you will see the day scene as painted (the fluorescent paint won't show up at all), but when you hit the drop with black light, it completely transforms and comes alive.

Examples of special effects devices made by L'Maitre
Provided by L'Maitre

The Broadway production of the *Guys and Dolls* revival, which was painted in very bright colors, used black lights throughout to give each set an extra punch.

Slides and computer-generated slide shows are very popular as scenic elements of late. Both *Evita* and *The Who's Tommy* use slides, and these can be rented along with the rehearsal material. You will mostly need a very powerful projector, such as one that uses a Xenon discharge lamp, if your theater is a large one, but in a small venue, simple Carousel types might work.

The key here is to keep ambient light off the screen. You can experiment with both front-screen and rear-screen projections; depending upon the distance, you can place the slide projector(s). You might also try a very wide-angle lens (the widest type called a fish-eye) so that the projector can be as close as possible (for brightness) and yet still give a big image.

Another, more sophisticated, way to go would be to use a graphic program on a computer to build a slide show, and then couple the laptop to a presentation projector—the type used for business presentations. A PC program such as Microsoft Power Point or a Mac program such as Macromedia's Director can create a wonderful multimedia "event," with dissolves and fades, utilizing drawings done in paint programs, images scanned into the computer, and even VHS or DVD footage.

For a staged reading of *Frankenstein, the Musical* that I co-authored, we used storyboards—the type used in preproduction of a movie—to add a visual to the actors who sat on stools. With the click of a button each image dissolved to the next one, giving the audience something fascinating to look at as well as to listen to.

A wonderful invention that I guess I would have to place under special effects is the Fiber Optic Star Curtain. This is a drop made of black material, lined (for protection), and with hundreds of polymer fibers sewn into it. The tip of these fibers are randomly spread across the drop and secured with a special adhesive. The intensity of the fiber point is controlled by its size, with .75 mm standard. A minimum of 2.25 points and a maximum of 3.75 points per square foot are usual. Any less would be ineffective; any more would be overpowering. The fiber strands are bundled together and terminate at the top center (although other configurations are possible) and the ends are connected in a bundle to an illuminator or even to many illuminators, which send the light down the fibers to create tiny points of light at the tips. Depending upon the configuration, you can change color, change twinkling speed, and even light up zones within the curtain. There is nothing more stunning than a Fiber Optic drop acting like a night sky—a thousand points of light twinkling away. While expensive, these can be rented as well, and designs can actually be created from the Fiber Optic points.

Chasers and rope lights are also special effect devices that can add sparkle (pun intended) to a production. Chasers are a string of sockets with tiny white or clear round bulbs. They are connected to a controller that, when activated, lights the bulbs sequentially creating a "chase sequence." The direction and the speed of the chase are variable; there is also a switch that turns them all on or all off. Chaser lights are often used around a marquee, around a proscenium, or around a passerale, emulating the burlesque or vaudeville runways. Lamp dip can colorize the bulbs.

Rope lights are even smaller lamps encased in a plastic tube that behaves like a chaser, only it is more "high-tech" looking. This item would not be used to give the feel of an old vaudeville house but rather as a decorative device unique to itself. As an example, we used rope lights inside the pinball machines used in the musical *The Who's Tommy*. Another example might be to outline a part of the set in a musical revue with rope lights of various colors, merely because it would add interest.

A look through the catalogs of theatrical supply houses will illustrate many of these special effects equipment and present you with new and interesting ways to use them.

Scenic Painting

The art of scenic painting can be a career choice. I'm not sure you can learn to be a great artist, but if you have any artistic skill at all, you can get away with basic scene painting.

In my experience I have found that the best bet is to employ or in some way coerce the services of an artist (maybe the art teacher at a local high school or a graphic artist from a local design business) to do the bulk of the work and to guide the other volunteers. It is always helpful to have "bodies" to do the base coating (painting the scenic units or drops white so that it takes the actual paint more effectively) and to copy an example set by the "charge" painter.

Drops are invariably the most difficult. They are done on such a large scale—they are in essence a huge mural—and the audience sees them for such a long time, that if you don't have an artist to paint them, you would be much better off renting them from a place such as Tobins Lake Studios (810-229-6666) or Grosh Scenic Studios (*www.grosh.com*) who have huge catalogs full of wonderful drops in various sizes. But if you do have someone who can conceive of a drop for you, then by all means, give it a try.

First you'll need muslin in a size for your theater. Muslin can be ordered in bulk and you can sew it, or you can order it ready to paint. The drop should have a two-inch bottom pocket or hem to house either a pipe to weight it and keep it taut if it is going to be flown in or to hold a chain if the drop is to travel on from the wings. The top needs to be finished in jute webbing, with grommets installed every foot along the length. Tie-line (the standard for theater, available in black or white) or S-hooks are used in the grommet holes to attach the drop to the carriers on a traveller track or to tie it to a dead-hung batten.

To sew such a drop and get the seams right, you need space and an industrial strength sewing machine. You'll also need space to paint the drop, as lying it out completely open is the best choice. You can do it in sections, but this is harder.

Before you can paint it with the scenic design you wish, the drop must be "sized" with a base coat of inexpensive white latex paint or sizing.

The easiest way to transfer a design from an elevation to the drop itself is by "gridding" it out. The design should paint a scale model of the drop on matte board in a half-inch scale, with as close to the colors as he envisions. Clear plastic or acetate is placed over the drop and half-inch squares are gridded onto it. Every half-inch square represents a square foot of the finished drop. Then, using chalk, grids are drawn on the muslin and each square is replicated in full scale.

With respect to paint, it has been my experience that paint designed specifically for theatrical use works best. It is meant to be watered down, from between one to two parts water for every one part paint, and it lasts longer—both on the muslin drops and flats, and on wooden set pieces—as well as in an open bucket. Theater paint comes in a limit of about eighteen colors and is meant to be mixed to specific shades. Art students are usually quite adept at mixing colors; I have known some who could match a Pantone chip exactly (Pantone is the standard for color in all aspects of the arts).

Example of a scenic drop elevation, drawn to scale, with grid
Designed by Vern H. Smith for Oliver!

Rosco makes a widely used line of scenic paints and has three separate varieties: Supersaturated Roscopaint, Iddings Deep Colors, and off-Broadway Scenic Colors. I have always preferred Iddings, but all are good and comparably priced. Experiment and find which works best.

You can also get white and black paint from Rosco, but here I have found that the deeply discounted brands from some of the Home Depot-type stores will work just as well in those two specific colors.

Theater paint can be put on with a variety of brushes or rollers or even with paint sprayers such as a Hudson Sprayer. And a variety of techniques can be employed, from straight painting to such effects as spattering, where you hold the brush and hit it against your hand to spatter color onto the flat or set. This is a very effective technique when you want to break up a flatly painted platform or set piece with some texture. Spattering, especially with two or three colors—some light and some dark—works very well because certain lights catch certain colors thus giving a dimensional look to flat scenery.

Another similar technique is rag rolling, where a bunched up rag is dipped in paint and rolled on the flats, giving texture. And dry brush techniques, where a small amount of paint is streaked across the flat with a stiff brush, make for successful wood grain and other surfaces.

Theater paint dries to a flat finish. If you want a glossy, lacquered look, try clear gloss latex, which is a white paint that dries clear and quite glossy, leaving the color underneath it to show through. We will often coat a stage floor with this paint (also called "Flo Paint"), although dancers sometimes complain that it makes for a slippery floor. Then we have to coat the glossy floor with two parts water, one part Coke or Pepsi, to make it sticky again. No joke.

Bronzing powder—which you must be careful with due to its toxicity—makes for a very metallic paint that can be used wherever you need a chrome, bronze, or gold look. (It's called Bronzing, but comes in aluminum, gold, copper, etc.)

As with all the elements of the set design and its accompanying props, a style must be determined. Usually it can be broken down between a choice of two—stylized or realistic.

If you choose stylized, then you have the freedom to let your imagination run amok. Buildings can be constructed without right angles so that they are askew. Props can be painted on to two-dimensional plywood cutouts. Bright and outrageous colors can be used where you wouldn't dare use them in real life. Sets and drops can be painted much more cartoon like. This technique has its place, especially in musicals such as *How To Succeed in Business . . .* , *Li'l Abner*, *Annie*, and other shows based on comics or fantasy stories. You can distort shadow and light and create a world that wouldn't exist in the real one.

Should you choose realism, which you most likely would for straight plays and serious musical subjects, then everything you do should be geared to making it look as much like life as possible.

This is yet another place where attention to detail pays off—you want to use texture, proper shadowing, molding, accessories, and above all, research to make sure what you come up with fits the period, the locale, and the class level of the characters—poor or rich, lower/middle/upper class, etc.

An additional thought—while this doesn't exactly fall under scene painting, there is also something called Rosco Colorine Lamp Dip, which comes in handy when you wish to change the color of light bulbs. Sometimes bare bulbs are incorporated into a set design—such as the chaser lights used in *Gypsy* or *Hello, Dolly!*—and if all you own are clear or white bulbs, you can use Lamp Dip to color the light bulbs, which give a unified and cohesive effect depending upon the colors of the set.

There are videotapes available that help describe scene-painting techniques, and those coupled with a good book are highly recommended.

Sound

Sound is the most difficult of all the disciplines. With all the other ones, you can see the result of your actions—does the light go on and does it light what it is supposed to—does the chair look the right color—will the platform hold the weight or not. The costume doesn't fit? Take it in or let it out.

Sound is different. It is invisible. You can hear if it is working, but if it is not, you can't readily see why.

The basic components of sound for the theater are:

Loudspeakers: usually a cluster of tweeters (for high end sounds), midrange speakers, and woofers and subwoofers for low-end sounds. They can be housed in fairly substantial and heavy speaker cabinets and suspended from the ceiling. Getting the proper angles—up and down tilts and left and right—can be tricky as there is a phenomenon where frequencies can disappear if the speakers' paths cross each other. It takes experimentation. Sometimes, like at rock concerts, they are piled up on the sides of the proscenium. If you have a balcony, you might need some up there as well.

Amplifiers: big industrial versions of the amps you have at home, often with more than 250 watts of power, powerful enough to drive the large loudspeakers. These are often kept in racks, away from electrical power and wires. Lots of cable will be needed to connect the speakers to the amps and the amps to the mixing board.

A sound mixer: a board that controls the volume of each microphone and often has other bells and whistles such as a graphic equalizer to custom fit the quality of the sound of each actor or instrument, and maybe some effects generators for reverb and echo. Small boards can have twelve or more sliders (also called "pots," short for potentiometer)—devices that raise and lower the volume of each item plugged into it, and more sophisticated boards can have many times that. The sound mixer also controls the volume of the sound effects and their minidisk players, MP3 players, CD-players, and even good old-fashioned cassette decks.

Two varieties of microphones may be used. The first style would be wired microphones, which are plugged directly into the mixing board and can be of several designs, such as shotguns, which pick up sounds a distance away; cardiod-style instrument mics; unidirectional floor mics, which can be used for ensembles and vocal groupings.

The second style would be wireless microphones. Wireless microphone systems are comprised of:

1. the miniature mic itself
2. a transmitter, which the performer wears concealed on his body
3. a wireless receiver, which has an antenna and is plugged into the mixing board

The wireless mics are the most problematic since they operate on different frequencies and can often pick up interference from radios, televisions, satellite dishes, police radios—you name it.

I strongly suggest that, if at all possible, you hire a professional to recommend and install your system and that you make sure you have someone who knows how to work everything—that sort of instruction is beyond the scope of this book. The remainder of this chapter, therefore, is going to be comprised of tips I have picked up over the years.

There's a song in one of the editions of *Forbidden Broadway* where the body mic is referred to as the Andrew Lloyd Webber disease. It seems that when the mega-musicals, imported from

London's West End, made their debut in New York City about twenty years ago, they brought with them the body mic, which can be seen now on most performers as a little black square over their ear or at the top of their forehead.

The body mic is certainly an improvement over the hand-held, wired mics that were used in the original production of *Hair*, and other rock musicals of the early 1970s, but they are not easy critters to tame. Here are a few tips we've discovered:

Placement of the little microphone element is very important. While they are often supplied with a tie-clip type device for a lapel or even a tie, putting the mic on clothing is risky as every little rustle comes across quite amplified. Better choices would be to fashion a half-circle out of a piece of wire and, using clear first aid tape, fasten the mic to the clip which is wrapped around the ear, like a hearing aid. An advantage here also is that the mic turns when the performer turns his head. Another good spot is under a wig, just peaking out at the top of the forehead.

Body mics come in both black and tan, and it is a good idea to have a variety of these elements on hand. You can use black when held in place by a wig, and black or tan if used on the ear.

Actors sweat a lot, and so plan on cleaning these elements after each performance and replacing them each season. There is a wire from the mic that has to run to the transmitter, which also is worn on the actor.

The costumers need to know if a body pack is being utilized, especially when the actor isn't wearing very much else. One safe way to house the transmitter, which is about the size of a pack of cigarettes, is by having the costumers make muslin pouches with flaps. These pouches are then sewn or pinned to a length of Ace bandage, and the butterfly clips that come with them can hold the bandage in place around the actor's waist. That's if the actor is wearing a regular costume.

I'll never forget the strippers in *Gypsy* having to wear their pouches in the back of their panties, or during *Little Shop of Horrors* when Audrey, in a tight mini skirt, wore her mic pack inside of her thigh.

The connecting cable between the mic and the transmitter should be secured to the body in a few places using Band-Aids. If the cord is visible, use invisible Band-Aids and use a flesh colored cord.

The sound engineer who is helping secure the body mics and packs should be the one who turns the pack on about a half-hour before the show. This should not be left to the performer.

Using a headset, the sound board operator should test each mic about fifteen minutes before curtain.

Body mics run on either 9-volt or AA batteries, which is an expense, because fresh ones MUST be used each night. Distortion results as the batteries run down. We recycle the batteries after each performance for other uses such as battery-powered candles, etc., since a battery that is not strong enough for a mic still has some use in it for other applications. We have also found that batteries stored in the fridge prior to use keep best.

To prevent moisture (such as sweat) from harming the expensive and delicate transmitters, it often pays to enclose them in a prophylactic. The sound folk often have a good time going into a drugstore and purchasing 100 at a time.

More often than not you'll find that you don't own enough body mic/transmitter combinations for all the performers who need them, and so you might have to swap between secondary characters. This is fraught with peril, so do it at your own risk. Certainly it is best if you have an intermission to do it, or a very long scene. In addition to all the trouble caused by costumes and Band-Aids, you'll need to make sure the volume sliders on the soundboard are properly marked so you know whose mic to activate.

Amplifying voices is certainly not the only use for sound in the theater. Sound effects and prerecorded music also have their place.

Playing appropriate music once the house is open (a half-hour before the curtain time usually) can help create the mood for the audience. I have used compilation CDs of Broadway overtures to get people in the mood for musicals or songs from the time period for straight plays. *Vanities* comes to mind as a show that almost has a running soundtrack throughout of "pop hits" from the various years the play scans. The recent Broadway revival of *One Flew Over the Cuckoo's Nest* made excellent use of weird, electronic music under the scenes of Chief Bromden's nightmarish monologues. I used the "Peer Gynt Suite" to accent a number of scenes in *Arsenic And Old Lace*.

All that is required is a CD player, an amplifier (even a consumer amp), and a couple of speakers. With CD burners readily available on most computers and the cost of blank CDs sometimes cheaper than audiocassettes, that is the format of choice for ease, reliability, and sound quality.

Here's a fun thing to try if the play calls for it:

For *The Hot L Baltimore*, the script calls for music to start playing over the house speakers before each act, and then as the lights fade to begin the scene, so does the music. But the music does not fade out; instead it cross-fades to appear to be coming from an old portable radio sitting behind the front desk of the old Hotel Baltimore. (If you've never seen the play, the title refers to the missing "e" in the neon sign outside the dilapidated hotel, which has been marked for demolition.) The way this is accomplished is to use a stereo map, but a mono recording of the music. One channel of the amp drives the house speakers; the other drives a tiny speaker hidden on stage, quite close to the prop radio. When the music has to dissolve from the house speakers to the stage speaker, you merely pan the stereo control from left (house speakers) to right (stage speakers) and adjust a volume as you do so. If you can feed everything through a mixing board, even better— you'll have more control and can even have the house speakers be stereo. This technique worked for *Lend Me A Tenor* and even for the musical *Mack and Mabel*, where the old-fashioned gramophone begins "I Won't Send Roses," and then the orchestra picks it up. Having a speaker on stage gives the audience a sense of where the music is emanating, rather than using the house speakers, which do not appear to be realistically coming from the stage.

Sound effects also benefit from "onstage" speakers set up throughout the set, or at least left and right of the proscenium. Listen to the sound effects on a good action movie played through your stereo system. The airplanes' roar travels left to right as the plane does; bullets appear to be fired from the same direction as the shooter; the telephone ring in the horror movie that startles both you and the unsuspecting heroine appears to come from the same side of the screen as the telephone. It is very effective to treat theater sound effects the same way: give them a direction.

The sound effects themselves can be obtained in a variety of ways. There are CDs available in stores and on the Internet with plenty of sound effects in the public domain—which means you can use them without royalties. Some websites exist with free sound effects that you can download. You can even "Foley" them, which is a movie term that originally referred to the artists who created the sound effects but now seems to be a cute way of describing any sound effect you create yourself with a microphone or a sampler or even a keyboard. A sampler—whether a stand-alone unit or one built into a keyboard—"samples" a sound you feed into it, via a microphone or from another prerecorded source—and then plays it back at the touch of a button or a keyboard key. This works very well for sound effects that are needed "on demand," such as gunshots.

All other sound effects can be burned to a CD (or a mini-disk) and played in order by cueing them up with a remote or right on the deck. This is a huge improvement over the days when audiocassettes were used for sound and you had to find your cues with a pair of headphones.

If you are good at the computer, you can build quite sophisticated sound effects by layering sounds on different tracks. There are a number of good software programs for just such purposes, for both PCs and Macs. For the staged reading of *Frankenstein, the Musical,* the lab sounds were comprised of over eight different overlapping tracks—Jacob's ladders, bubbling noises, rain, thunder and lightning, arc welders, sparks—all mixed together.

Sound effects, judiciously used, add life to a show, and you should consider not only those called for in the script (broken glass or telephone rings) but also running ambient sounds, such as traffic noise or thunderstorms, underneath a scene can really heighten reality.

Intercom Systems

The final technical area left to discuss is a subset of sound. Theaters often can make great use of an intercom system, connecting the lighting booth to the backstage area, with extensions to the follow spot operators, sound board, and even dressing rooms.

The standard for the industry is made by Clear-Com, although there are other manufacturers out there, such as Telex and Production Intercom. The two-way communication system consists of a main station with two or four channels, a power supply, digital belt packs (receiver/transmitters), and headsets with microphones, both wired and wireless.

The main station is mounted somewhere in your theater, most likely where you keep your other sound equipment. Cables are run to sound connections throughout the theater—wherever there is a need for communication. The receiver/transmitters plug into the connections via XLR (a 3-pin audio connector), and the headsets plug into packs. Now the stage manager can speak to the shift crew, the board operator, the spot operators— in fact anyone who needs to communicate quietly during the show. There can even be a "squawk box" permanently set up somewhere in the theater where the director, producer, or whomever can speak to everyone on headset.

Based on the way you have the system configured, the people on headset can reply to the stage manager or to each other, or their units can be rendered mute.

The wireless units allow backstage crew to move freely— perhaps while changing the set—and still hear their cues or commands.

Radio Shack and other manufacturers sell consumer-grade FM wireless headsets. These can work in a pinch, but because of FM interference in the sets themselves, as well as interfering potentially with your wireless body mics, these are not optimum.

Regardless of how sophisticated or powerful a system you install, some sort of intercom is pretty much imperative in all but the smallest of theaters.

The Director

While the great majority of this book was written while wearing my producer's hat, I have also directed over 100 plays and musicals during my life in the theater, so I thought it appropriate to share some directing thoughts with you.

While the buck ultimately stops with the producer/president/board of directors—their name is generally the first one above the title or the last one under the artistic staff—the director helms the day-to-day creation of a show.

Research

One of the best words of advice I can give to the director is to be prepared and do your research and homework. The actors and creative staff are going to look to you for answers to a myriad of questions—from "what is my motivation in this scene" to "do you want a loveseat or a sofa"–and the more you know the material, the easier these questions will be to answer.

When I accept the assignment of directing a show, my first task is to read the script—or reread it if it is a show I have directed before. The first pass I make through the libretto (if it is a musical or playscript if it is not) is more a visceral one. I just want to get a feel for the piece, and I make notations on my initial reactions. Perhaps there is a passage that strikes me as being confusing, or maybe I get inspired on how to stage a certain scene.

If this is a musical, there is a second step that you can skip if you are working on a straight play. For musicals, I will next turn to the original cast album of the show and give it an initial listen, again making notes—either mental or literal—on things that I react to.

The original cast album of most shows differs—either subtly or drastically—from the script and score that you can license. Measures will be missing from individual songs. Tempos will have been changed to "sound" more pleasing to a listener rather than to a viewer. Whole songs might be gone. Certainly most of the incidental and underscoring music will be missing. The underscore and incidental music refer to such things as music written to be played while scenery is being changed, short reprises that occur, and musical passages or vamps of measures that are repeated underneath dialogue.

A vamp is one or two measures of a short passage of music that can be repeated as a safety while dialogue is being spoken, scenery is moved into place, or lights fade up or down. It would sound irritating and redundant on a recording without the visual that accompanies it.

If you have some experience with reading music it is a good idea to listen to the cast album while following along in the piano/conductor's score. The piano/conductor's score is provided with the rehearsal material or perusal copies you receive from the licensing house, and it is more or less a "reduction" of the entire orchestration, designed to be played by an accompanist on a piano. Some shows also contain an additional score that the conductor will use when leading the orchestra during performances; others expect the conductor to use the Piano/Conductor score.

If you find significant discrepancies between the script, score, and cast album, then one of your resource projects begins. You will want to seek out material that is closer to the script and score made available to you.

I can give you a concrete example. The version of *Jekyll & Hyde* that MTI leases is not the Broadway version, but rather the post-Broadway tour version. Entire songs have been replaced from those on the original cast album from the Broadway production.

When comparing the score to the cast album, I knew I would have to do further research. I went on the Internet and discovered there were a number of other *Jekyll & Hyde* recordings on compact disk. There was a two-disk "concept album" that listed some of the songs I was looking for from the production script I had. I bought that album, and between the two, I was able to mix and match a recording that closely resembled what I had to work with. This was a help not only to myself as the director but also to the choreographer and musical director.

Additionally, there was a legitimate videotape production available on tape and DVD of David Hasselhoff appearing in *Jekyll & Hyde* that I also bought. While this too differed greatly from the published script, it was of tremendous help in suggesting the costumes and props to the staff.

So here is a list of resources that you should try and find first when contracted to direct a show.

An Original Broadway Cast album

The original Broadway cast album or the original London cast album (sometimes available as an import) is in most instances a somewhat truncated version of the musical, recorded with the original cast. If you are really resourceful in your research, you can often find cast albums from other countries as well. I believe I have somewhere an Israeli version of *Blood Brothers*.

A Concept Album of the Entire Score

A *concept album*, is a recording in which a group of performers— sometimes rather well known—get together to a make what is usually a two-disk set of virtually the entire score, including incidental music. It might be before the show is actually produced, such as the first versions *Jesus Christ, Superstar* and *Tommy*, or it might be years after the show has closed but was never fully preserved by the original cast album. If one is available, by all means buy it. Some that come to mind are: *My Fair Lady* with Jonathan Price, *Cabaret* with Greg Edelman, and *West Side Story* with a primarily operatic cast.

The Movie Version of the Show

In days gone by most hit shows were turned into movies. Movies tend to be very different (Fosse's *Cabaret, Evita*) from the show version but occasionally they are fairly faithful (*Li'l Abner, My Fair*

Lady, Oliver!). Either way, they are valuable for a sense of the period, for the props, for the costumes, and for the local color. Hollywood spends fortunes on that sort of detail.

A Videotape Version of the Actual Live Performance

This is the most helpful: occasionally there are video versions created of the actual stage show aired on PBS or Showtime, and then made available on tape or DVD. Among the titles that fall under this category: *Pippin, Jekyll & Hyde; The Royal Family; Joseph and the Amazing Technicolor Dreamcoat; Cats; Jesus Christ, Superstar.* There have also been a number of made-for-television versions of shows and musicals that are helpful: Bette Midler in *Gypsy*, Jason Alexander in *Bye Bye Birdie*, Kathy Bates in *Annie*, and even Marjoe Gortner in *The Robber Bridegroom.*

Check out *www.broadwayarchive.com/*. This website has the most complete collection of actual plays and musicals on tape and DVD for sale.

There are also shows that were movies first, then made into Broadway shows, and the original source material can provide a wealth of research material. Examples include: *Footloose, Saturday Night Fever, King of Hearts, Sunset Boulevard, Meet Me In St. Louis, Fame,* and *The Sweet Smell of Success*, as well as plenty of nonmusicals.

While we're talking research, an ambitious and efficient director will also seek out resources that are not necessarily directly related to the show but that evoke the period, the costumes, the history—to get a feel for the flavor of the piece. This research is available everywhere—on the Internet, in the library, in similar movies and recordings. Immersing yourself in the genre of the show will go a long way toward making you an authority on it—which is exactly what the director needs to be.

Preproduction Work on the Script

The next step is to revisit the script. On this pass-through, you might start to envision some of the "stage pictures" you wish to create and some of the actor's blocking. A stage picture is generally a "look" you create for an actor or a group of actors—perhaps you envision the leading character standing downstage center while the ensemble forms a semicircle behind her. Using a series of *X*s and arrows and circles—whatever you are comfortable with—you can make diagrams in the margins of the script that will help you later on, when you are standing in front of the actors telling them what to do.

This is called creating your preproduction script. Directors work in a great many different ways. I am used to directors who will write in every piece of blocking beforehand—even working it out with chess pieces on a floor plan. Their script would be filled with penciled-in commands such as:

> *X DS L* (cross downstage left) or *G enter R1 X exit L2* (girls enter "in one" from the right and cross to exit left in two). Add a series of arrows and circles to define traffic patterns and the script might resemble a football coach's diagram of plays.

This results in a very confident director who can approach the day's rehearsal with assurance. Having a road map of this sort also gives the actors great assurance that they are in the hands of a director who is on top of the material. This does not mean that if something happens organically on stage that it cannot be utilized—that's what pencils and erasers are for.

Other directors plan much less in advance. They will know where entrances and exits are to occur or when and where people might sit, but they will leave a great deal to the inspiration of the moment and the actor's instincts. After the scenes are run a few times, they will "cement" the blocking based on what worked best. "Cementing" a moment or even an entire show means that everyone is to assume nothing further will change—it is set in stone, to extend the metaphor.

Still other directors work completely in an improvisational manner, leaving it all up to the moment and cementing it many rehearsals later. This is good in a workshop, a theater class, or when working on a new piece, but when time is of the essence it is not the most practical.

Whichever style you use, or how you combine the styles, should be determined to some degree by the actors you are using. If you are working with performers with whom you have worked extensively in the past, it is sometimes possible to allow for more freedom. You can sense what they can be counted on to do and they would instinctively have a sense of what you are looking for. But if this is a new group, especially of less experienced performers, it is often best to come as prepared as possible.

My personal style is to block a skeletal version of the scene that I have prepared prior to rehearsal and then watch it a few times in succession. The actors will start to experiment, and new ideas will hit me. I will then revise the scene and run it a few more times, revising further as needed. Eventually, by the end of rehearsal, I will ask the actors to commit to this version until told otherwise.

Working with Actors

Interestingly, there seem to be two types of actors. There are those who, once you tell them to freeze something (meaning to commit to it), have a devil of a time making revisions. If they rehearse a scene standing midstage, for instance, and three weeks later you tell them to move the scene more downstage, it'll take another week of constant reminding to get them to do it.

Other actors are perfectly adaptable—they have become proficient in their ability to adapt to whatever is thrown at them. This is, of course, less frustrating for the director.

It is often helpful to announce at the first rehearsal what style you are going to adopt for this particular show. While not everyone will be able to adhere to your style, at least you have warned them of what they can expect.

Getting the most out of an actor is an art that a director must embrace. This is not a put down of actors—I have been one myself—but they are often fragile, needy creatures with either humongous egos or none at all. The acting experience and the creation of a character make them quite vulnerable, and they need the director to coach them through the process of becoming a whole new person on stage. The director is their mirror, and they must trust him or her and believe in their Director for it all to work out. Sometimes the character they portray is foreign to them, and they need guidance; sometime it is very close to them, and they need perspective.

You will meet and work with all sorts of actors. There are those who treat theater as a craft and come to rehearsal prepared to work professionally—to learn and to create.

Others treat it as a vocation or hobby. They hold other jobs, which sometimes take their attention and distract them. Many have not been trained in producing results in the most efficient manner—but they want to learn and want to develop their skills. This is the actor you will come across most often.

Then there are the actors who are in the show for less than artistic reasons—for the parties, for the social interaction, or any number of other reasons. They can be challenging, as their attention span sometimes is a tad limited.

The most effective directors can call upon a grab bag of resources in dealing with each type of actor that they work with.

Obviously you want to be understanding, compassionate, and supportive of every performer. But when you are working with semi-pros, you can work in a much more efficient manner, using verbal short cuts to get your direction across. They often need fewer explanations of your notes and can give you what you are looking for in a short amount of time—which is helpful as time is usually of the essence.

The good old reliable average community theater actor needs a bit more handholding. I often find that they are sincere in their willingness to produce good results, and I am happy to discuss my notes and my reasoning with them. Rather than giving them a class in Acting 101, I feel I am helping them to develop their personal style and craft. I give more when they give back.

The following is a paraphrased version of a speech I have made on a number of occasions: "We have all joined together here with a single purpose—to produce the best play within our means. Therefore, I must ask each and every actor to commit themselves to that purpose for the hours they are here for rehearsal. It doesn't affect me if you socialize before you get here or afterwards—but when you are here I expect your total concentration. You have made the commitment, so for the three hours that you are here a night, you are mine, and I expect your cooperation."

I have certainly had to ask a terribly unruly and distracting actor to leave the company, but that is the exception to the rule.

Going back to an earlier statement, if you cast the show well, right from the beginning, your job is well on its way to a successful conclusion.

Theater Games and Acting Exercises

If you have the time, there are certain theater games and acting exercises that you can utilize to help the actors develop their characters and to encourage a bonding among the actors. Creating a connection between what are oftentimes total strangers is a challenge that these exercises address. Dramas and comedies lend themselves to this sort of activity far more than musicals, where often you are not given the stage time to fully explore your character—in fact, sometimes the characters in musicals are written rather two-dimensionally, although you should never play them that way.

Two areas to explore with your actors are their past lives and their subtext. Exercises in past lives requires the actor to develop a biography for their character, giving some thought to who they are, where they came from, how they were educated, who their family was—anything and everything that makes them behave in the way that they do when you finally get to see them on stage.

You can ask each actor to write up their character's background, or maybe explain themselves to the other cast members— this latter method is a way for the other actors to gain insight into each other. This is one of the joys of working on a straight play— the chance to submerge oneself into someone else and completely become a new personality. I remember working on the role of Teach in *American Buffalo* when I was younger—a sleazy, low-life character if there ever was one, and I found that it alienated many of my friends who found me intolerable during the rehearsal period.

Exploring the subtext is to delve between the lines—to take what the characters are saying and consider what their motivation might be. An actor can ask themselves "why am I saying this?" or "why am I behaving in this manner," and in doing so, he will find clues as to how to portray the character fully. The director's job here is to guide the actors in their road to discovery.

There are also improvisations and warm-ups that can be useful tools if time allows. I am not a huge fan of these exercises—I prefer to jump right into the script itself, but if they suit your style, there are plenty of books on the subject.

Thoughts on Staging

In the past few years I have concentrated more on staging musicals than directing comedies and dramas and have learned a number of techniques that hopefully make for a more interesting production. Some of these suggestions involve the work of the choreographer, and as I have stated before, the best musicals tend to blur the line between what is staging and what is dancing.

If your forte is the nonmusical, I would hope these concepts could be applied to your work as well.

I have always felt that there needs to be a strong connection between the set designer and the director. Given the opportunity, I often try and design the sets for shows I am directing. In instances where I am designing for another director, or am using a set designer other than myself, I try to communicate and share ideas right from the start. So much of the staging of a show is dependent on the proper and creative use of the set. The opposite is true as well—if a set designer fully understands how a director wishes to utilize a set, then the designs can be created accordingly.

If you conceive of the proscenium as a frame, then what happens on the stage can be thought of as a picture within that frame. And like any work of art, that picture should have elements of composition and harmony. In addition, the director and choreographer are working not only in two dimensions like a painter would be but also in three dimensions, utilizing the depth of the stage for their compositions. While a painting is frozen in time, stage pictures are usually fluid, changing often within a scene, as well as between scenes. Scene shifts should be considered artwork as well, especially if those changes are made au vista (in view of the audience).

Some of the elements of staging that should be considered are:

- Focus—who or what is the main visual element of the scene. If it is the leading character, then you must consider the actor's placement. Dead center, facing the audience, will command more focus than upstage left. If the actor is standing on something taller than the other actors, that will command attention, even if they are not dead center. A lighting "special" will emphasize the leading character. If everyone else on stage is looking at the leading character, their focus will cause the audience to focus on the same subject as well.

■ Balance—this is especially important when dealing with an ensemble, but it holds true with a smaller group of actors as well. Unless there are reasons dictating for you to do otherwise, spreading people out to make a pleasing composition is something to strive for. Not only spreading them out left to right, but front to back, and, if the set allows, on varying heights.

Never let the ensemble stand in a straight line, unless you are doing *A Chorus Line*. Bunch them up and vary their upstage/downstage depth. This is both more realistic and more pleasing.

For the production of *Jekyll & Hyde* that I directed and Michelle Massa choreographed, I designed the set as well, because the director in me had a concept that would only work if the set designer supported it. It was my idea that the ensemble, which represents the "haves" and the "have-nots" of London in 1888, remain on stage throughout most of the show, reacting to what is going on and often providing a visual counterpoint to it. This would only work if there were many levels for them to inhabit to prevent redundancy in the staging and choreography. So I created an environment that contained a revolving stage, two-level platforms stage left and stage right, and a large bridge that connected the platforms midstage, twelve feet up off the revolve.

The actors were able to walk, crawl, and climb all over the set, creating a different and interesting visual composition for each scene.

The revolve worked very well—not only did it enable us to change the set pieces fluidly by loading them on to the revolve upstage and revolving them downstage—but having groups of actors walk in one direction while the revolve turned in opposition provided a striking image.

Yet another aside: we built the revolve, which was twenty-one feet in diameter and eight inches thick, like an eight-slice

The half-inch model of *Jekyll & Hyde*
Designed by Gary P. Cohen

pizza. Since our stage is somewhat uneven, we found it was best to cover the slices with wood on the bottom as well as on the top and place the casters on the deck of the stage upside down. In this manner we could adjust the height of the casters to account for the unevenness of the floor. Another added advantage is that a stray screw or nail would not get caught under the casters. If you are having trouble envisioning this, maybe the image of a revolving tray in a microwave oven will help—these trays rest on wheels that are on the bottom of the microwave.

Keep in mind when blocking your show that certain sections of the stage hold more weight—figuratively, not realistically—and you can use that to your advantage. Entering from stage right is more powerful than doing so from stage left. Entering upstage and walking downstage is more powerful than entering and moving on the same level. Downstage center is most powerful; right center is more powerful than left center.

A staging device you might wish to incorporate into your own work is to build each scene or dance.

To elaborate, I'll give you the example of the title song, which closes Act I (spectacularly I might add) of the musical *Mame*. Musically and visually the number keeps building and building, even though the melody basically stays the same. One technique used was to have three people execute a specific step, then three more people were added to the same step, then eight more were added. While the step itself may not be terribly showy, by building and building the number of people it became most impressive and garnered applause every performance. The structure of the number was such that small groups of dancers would perform specific dance combinations, followed by yet another group. This allowed the choreography to feature the various strong points of individual dancers. Changing the style and look of the dancers varied the number further: a line step was followed by a circle step; a left-to-right step was followed by a front-to-back step. And of course, the number climaxed with that old applause-assuring move—the kick line.

Composers use the device of a key-change to build a song to a powerful conclusion, and directors and choreographers must find methods to do the same with their staging.

An obvious method would be to bring more and more people on stage as the scene or the number progresses. Another might be to start a number upstage and slowly bring it downstage (the Act I conclusion of *Les Miz* does this). Simple choreography that gets more and more elaborate achieves the effect of building excitement. A scene that begins low key—in lighting, vocally, physically—and grows in intensity will keep the audience's attention far longer than a scene that stays at the same excitement level throughout.

I also believe musical numbers should evolve realistically out of the style of the show. By this I refer to making it appear that the dancers—whether ensemble or leading players—are motivated to dance by their circumstance. *My Fair Lady*, for example, allows for this method. In addition to the waltzing done at the Embassy Ball, which is entirely motivated by the plot device, Alfred Doolittle's two songs—"With a Little Bit of Luck" and "I'm Getting Married in the Morning"—allow for dancing that is entirely character based. Doolittle, his friends, and the Cockney townspeople begin to dance because it is the next logical step in their excitement of being caught up in the moment. And when they do dance, their steps are entirely realistic within the nonrealistic world of musical comedy.

When we settle into our seats to watch a musical, we immediately suspend our belief and accept a world where people will break out and sing, and sometimes dance, even when they are at death's door. This goes with the territory, and we buy it. But the dances must still seem to fit the period and style of the play—the dancing performed in the two songs from *My Fair Lady* mentioned previously appear "organic." The dancers are doing steps that seem within the reach and realm of their station in life and the time period. The dancing is entirely "appropriate."

It is also effective to use props and set pieces in the dancing and staging. In *My Fair Lady*, the flower cart becomes essential to Eliza's "Wouldn't It Be Loverly." Susan Stroman, one of modern theater's great director/choreographers, made using props into a science in such shows as *Crazy for You* (ropes turned into basses, dancing on tin roofs) and *The Producers* (note the old ladies with the walkers).

When staging and/or choreographing a play or musical, embracing the details holds true for both the director and the choreographer. You can have a wonderful and varied set, lit beautifully, with actors in stunning costumes handling the most realistic props, but if your staging is bland or your choreography is inappropriate, then you don't have much of a show.

Theater Essentials

After so many years' experience, I offer this list of items that should be kept in good supply at your theater. Production people sometimes keep many of these items (the smaller ones, of course) in what they call a "Gak box"—so that they, like the Boy Scouts, are always prepared.

Items to Keep on Hand

- "Littllite"—a small, intense light that either can be attached to lighting and sound boards or can stand alone on its own base for use on a production table during tech week. Invaluable when you are taking notes.

- Drafting templates—a must for drawing light plots, they are plastic rectangles available in half-inch and quarter-inch scale and contain stencils, templates of lighting symbols, furniture symbols, and scenic elements for use in drawing and drafting.

- Flashlights—have plenty of these around. Theater is created in darkened spaces, and flashlights are essential. Backstage crews should carry them to help actors navigate into the wings on their exits and entrances.

- Gel swatch books—little three-inch by one-and-a-half-inch examples of every gel color and diffusion filters grouped together in a handy package, put out by Rosco, Gam, and other companies. Most companies reissue new versions every three years.

- Fabric swatch books—all types of fabric and color samples in a handy package, put out by companies such as Rose Brand.

- Hot glue guns and sticks of hot glue—a must for the prop shop, but also good for set decoration and quick repairs.

- Lighting equipment testing tools—such as the GamCheck series, which allow electricians to check polarity, lamp and fixture continuity, and all other problems that can occur.

- Walkie-talkies—helpful when focusing lights and in other situations where the crew is spread throughout the theater.

- Gaffer's tape—a cloth utility tape with a zillion purposes. It comes in black (the most useful), white, gray, and yellow. Generally, the most useful is the two-inch-wide variety, sold in sixty-yard rolls, but you can also get it in one- and three-inch widths. Do not confuse it with duct tape, even though they are both the same size and come on rolls. Duct tape, while great for your basement, has little use in theater. Gaffer's tape is the tape to use in every department.

- Spike tape—a cloth, paper, or vinyl tape, available in a multitude of colors, that is used to make marks on the stage so that crew members know where to place set pieces, actors know where to stand, and areas of the stage can be defined. A stage manager will often make a ground plan out of spike tape of the set design on the floor of the rehearsal space during the rehearsal period—until the real set is constructed or until the actors move into the real theater. Yellow or orange show up the best, and cloth, in my opinion, is preferable. Spike tape, if pulled up within a reasonable period, will not leave a residue on the stage floor. Spike tape is also sold in precut corners, for "spiking" furniture. Very cute and helpful.

- Glow tape—a luminescent tape that glows in the dark after being subjected to stage lights. It is used to mark the stage or stairs or platforms for actors to maneuver on in a blackout.

- Double-faced tape—a two-sided adhesion tape for hidden bonding. Can keep a toupee in place!

- Safety tape and cable path—a two-inch-wide roll of tape, in bold black and yellow slanted stripes, meant to warn actors of cables, low hanging lights, and other potential dangers. Cable path is similar, but is four or six feet wide, and the center is nonadhesive so that it allows a tunnel for cables.

- Curtain or clothing steamer—removes wrinkles from most drapery and clothing quickly via steam.

- Grommets, grommet hole cutter, and setting dies and hammer—grommets are small metal circles that you install into the tops of curtains to make rip-proof paths for tie-line. The hole cutter cuts the clearance in the curtain, the setting dies and hammer fuse the two halves of the grommet itself.

- Tie-line, also called trick line—a thin, braided cotton or poly rope, sold on a 3,000-foot reel, used for a great many theatrical purposes including hanging lightweight scenery on a batten, tying back curtains, "dressing" cables (making them look clean) on a pipe, and for operating some special effects. Basically it is the gaff tape of rope. It comes in black and white.

- Wagon brakes—a quick-release brake that is screwed on to rolling platforms (also known as wagons) that provides secure holding power.

Depending upon what department you are working in, you might want to invest in some of the following tools and supplies: scissors, pliers, hammers, various sizes of Phillips and slotted screwdrivers, Allen keys, assorted sizes of adjustable Crescent wrenches, lineman pliers, needle nose pliers, adjustable channel-lock pliers, crimping pliers, pipe (Stilson) wrench, chalk, and chalk line, magic markers, baling wire, zip ties, measuring tapes (up to twenty-five feet at least), pens and pencils and pencil sharpeners, utility knife, safety pins, bobby pins, and just about anything else that might come in handy.

Additional Concerns to Address

Fire Codes

Any venue that is open to the public will be subject to rather stringent fire codes. You can expect a visit from the local fire department when you first open and every year or so thereafter. Some of their concerns will be:

Abundant fire extinguishers throughout the building, checked yearly. There are different types for different emergencies—you will most likely want to have a variety on hand.

Your exits have to be clearly marked with lighted signs. Access to the exits has to be clear. If you are in a Black Box space there might be some restrictions as to where you can have your seating.

Nothing can be stored around any electrical boxes, particularly the area housing the feed from the street. There will be codes addressing emergency turn-off switches as well.

If you have a sprinkler system, there are codes dictating how close props, costumes, and other items can be stored in proximity to the ceiling.

Flammable paint—such as oil-based paints, deck enamel, turpentine, and spray paint—might have to be kept in a vented area.

Your soft goods will have to be fire retardant in most cases.

The list goes on, so the best bet would be to invite the fire marshall in to go over the applicable codes. This way you won't be caught off guard. While there is a grace period in which to correct infractions, failure to do so could result in being shut down or fined.

Insurance

You will want to make sure you are sufficiently covered for theft, fire, and most certainly, liability. You are in a business where you ask your actors to do things where they might get hurt—dancing, climbing, jumping, acrobatics, using props—and people can get hurt. You are in a business where construction takes place and technicians are asked to climb heights, use power tools, handle electrics—and people can get hurt. You are in a business where there is an audience—and people can get hurt. Make sure you are sufficiently insured and that you are not personally responsible. Make this priority one before you even open the doors.

Accidents

What to do in the event of an accident? Stay levelheaded and act quickly. The number of the local First Aid Squad should be posted

by every phone in the theater. Don't take any chances; send someone to call them first.

You should have on hand several first aid kits, stocked with
all the essentials. It is also good to stock a box or two of "Instant
Cold Packs"—which provide an ice effect when smacked on a hard
surface. Injuries to dancers can be helped with a cold pack until
the squad arrives.

If anyone connected with the theater is trained in first aid,
it wouldn't hurt for them to hold an informal training session
with your staff. I can't say it enough—make safety a major concern—for your audience and your volunteers.

Parking Problems

You want to make parking as convenient as possible. Many people, especially seniors, have concerns if they park a distance from
the theater. Make sure you have the proper amount of accessible
parking spots, properly marked. Consult the ADA or your state's
ADA advisory organization. For example, New Jersey has the Arts
Access Task Force, which is specifically designed to handle the concerns of arts organizations.

If your building has its own parking lot, all the better. Just make
sure it is well lit and well maintained. If not, perhaps you might be
able to make some sort of arrangement with a public parking lot for
special discounts on performance nights for your audience. If all you
have are metered spots on the street, you might try and make a deal
with another local store that has parking but is closed at night.

However you attack the issue, try to make it as simple and
as easy as possible for your audience to get to you.

The Many Uses for Computers

I have a love/hate relationship with my computers (a desktop PC,
laptop, and two Macs) because I use them for hours on end on a
daily basis. When they function as they should, they are the great-
est invention of the twentieth century. When they crash and ruin
hours of work, they are expensive paperweights. But love them or
hate them, they are invaluable to the theater.

Here are some of the uses I have found for computers.

Word Processing and Database Projects

- Press releases—I have created a template with a heading that reads: NEWS—FOR IMMEDIATE RELEASE.

- Correspondence—another template with our letterhead.

- Databases of our lighting, set, prop, and costume inventory. Created in Microsoft Excel, these databases contain the item, the amount in stock, where the item is stored, details on the item, and best of all, a digital photo. It took ages to compile, but it was worth the effort. If I want to know if we have a walking stick, for example, I type in "canes" into the Prop Database, and up comes a photo of any and all we have in stock.

- Audition notes—I sit at auditions with my laptop.

- Production notes—I sit at rehearsals with my laptop and then print out the notes.

- Production calendars—invaluable—I give them to every staff member.

- Rehearsal schedules.

The list goes on and on.

Email and Internet

Email is a wonderful way to communicate—it is quick and environment friendly. I am constantly addressing questions from people who have visited our website and want info on shows, audiences, directions, you name it. Another technological marvel is to create a Group Contact List in your email program for categories of people—crew, casts of shows, creative staffs—this way you can send out a bulk mailing to each group in one shot. I also talk with vendors via email and place orders conveniently.

The Internet has two major purposes for me (aside from stock quotes, movie times, and the weather). First, I use it for the theater website; second, I use it for research and purchases.

Having a presence for your theater on the World Wide Web makes it very simple to promote your season and let people know all of the ins and outs of your facility.

Virtually every major supplier of theater goods has a website, and most often they are full of insight into not only their products but also theater information in general.

Drawing and Design Programs

From the simplest drawing program to sophisticated programs such as AutoCAD, the computer is a great way to create prop, set, and lighting designs. What used to be done by hand can be automated and tedious steps such as repeatedly drawing twenty Fresnels on a batten can be done quickly with "cut and paste" functions. Copies can be easily printed out as well. A software program such as Lightwright is invaluable to the lighting designer, as the program will generate circuit and patching charts, instrument schedules, gel counts, and hanging plots. If you are into lighting, check out *www.mckernon.com.*

Ticketing Software

Many companies sell the software to automate your ticket-selling process via a computer. It can handle seating charts, future sales, group sales, mailing lists—anything and everything to make the box office run smoothly.

Love 'em or hate 'em, computers are here to stay, and they can make your life in the theater a little bit easier. You might even use a computer to write a book or a script, as I have.

Conclusion

I hope this book has provided an interesting and informative read. Writing it was a revelation for me, as it forced me to look at the work I have done for the past thirty-five-plus years and evaluate it. The old adage—if I knew then what I know now—certainly is true enough. My days with Celebration Playhouse were naïve and full of mistakes, but without those mistakes I never would have learned so much. Certainly running a small community theater and handling almost all the jobs myself paved the way to being hired to supervise a much larger venue successfully.

If this book can stop the fledgling producer/president/artistic director from making some of the mistakes I made, then my book will have value. And if the established producer/president/artistic director discovers a trick or a shortcut to making his or her job easier or the theater run more smoothly, then that would be wonderful as well.

I don't mean to be corny or maudlin, but the bottom line is—to run a community theater, you really need to be in love with theater. It has to be in your blood.

It is an all-consuming job. You wake up in the middle of the night to jot down ideas or make notes on things that might not have gone so well at that evening's rehearsal. You can't get some song from the show you are working on out of your head, and it drives you berserk. You subsist on pizza and burgers, soda and snacks. You show up to work with a fever or a sore throat or a splitting headache. You believe, above all, that the show must go on.

However, the reward you get is a feeling of jubilation when the audience responds positively to your work. Each show is like a child growing up, and there's nothing more satisfying than being a proud parent.

No matter what size venue you are connected with, and no matter what type of shows you produce, as long as you create to the best of your ability then you will be making a valid contribution to the world of community theater in your little part of the world.

In this age of technology—of computers and DVDs and "reality" TV (a trend that hopefully will pass soon)—live theater is not on the top of everyone's to do list. But for those of us who believe that there is nothing more exciting than a wonderfully performed musical or straight play with living actors right in front of us, we have a duty to make sure theater is available in every community. We need to provide it, perform it, and promote it. For our own satisfaction and for the satisfaction of our audience.

And we need to remember the details.

Glossary

Apron: the stage area that extends in front of the proscenium, often curved.

Batten: a metal pipe, one or two inches in diameter, suspended above the stage and running the length of the stage, that holds scenery and lighting instruments. Also referred to simply as a "pipe."

Black box: a simple theater space that is completely flexible in terms of where the staging area is and where the audience sits.

Blocking: the movement of the actors on stage: when they sit, when they stand, when they cross downstage, when they exit, etc.

Book musical: a musical that has a script, as opposed to a Rock Opera such as *Les Miz* or *Jesus Christ, Superstar.*

Color scroller: a device that sits in the gel frame holder of a lighting instrument, containing a roll of gel of various colors. Through a DMX connection to a lighting board, the operator can set the scroller to move through the various colors and stop at the one required. This allows one lighting instrument to act as many in terms of color.

Control console or lighting board: a device that electronically or manually controls the dimmer modules, which in turn control the brightness of the lighting instruments, from fully on to off. Modern computer boards can also "memorize" cues, which control lots of lights at the same time. Older theaters might be equipped with a "dimmer board," which is an electromechanical control attached directly to the dimmers where they form banks of controls.

Cyber-light (brand name HIGH END CYBERLIGHT): also used a generic term for a moving light, is a lighting instrument that is electronically controlled by the control console. It can rotate and pan, change colors and gobos, and zoom in and out.

Cue: cues can mean a number of things: something that dictates an actor's entrance or for an actor to begin speaking; something that dictates that something technical is to happen such as a set shift or a special effect that is to be executed; a set of commands entered into a lighting board that controls the lighting on the stage. Warning cues tell the operator to "stand by"; the go cue means to execute the command.

Cue-to-cue: refers to a rehearsal where the technical people ask the actors to speed through the script, stopping only when something technical is involved—light cues, set shifts, prop hand-offs, and the like.

Cyc: short for cyclorama, a seamless piece of fabric, often white but also available in light blue or light green, which covers the entire back wall of a theater and is often used as a sky. Some cycs are hung on semicircular tracks.

Dead hung: when a curtain, drop, or other piece of scenery is tied to a batten that cannot raise or lower.

Deck: refers to the stage floor.

DMX: a new type of standard control protocol between the lighting control console (the lighting board) dimmers, instruments, and accessories.

Doubles: refers to a musician playing two or more instruments as dictated by a specific score.

Dressing the set: means to add the details that make it a real, believable environment, such as lamps, furniture, molding, wallpaper, rugs, ad infinitum.

Drops: scenery painted on to muslin and suspended from a batten.

Dry-tech: a tech rehearsal held only for the deck people—the actors are not called in.

Downstage: the area of the stage closest to the audience and the act of moving towards the edge of the stage.

Ellipsoidal reflector spotlight or profile spot (sometimes also called a Leko, which is actually the brand name for a Lekolite by Strand, but has become a generic term): a spotlight that uses an ellipsoidal reflector and can be easily focused. Can be used for "specials" and accepts gobos, gels, and color scrollers.

Ensemble: the actors in a musical, who are not leads or support-ing, sometimes called the chorus. A group of leading actors in a play whose roles are more or less equal. A matching outfit.

Fly space, fly loft, or flies: the area above the stage, typically twice the height, where entire pieces of scenery can be lifted and stored. A drop hanging on a batten and stored forty feet above the stage, can then be "flown in"—meaning it is low-ered into the view of the audience.

Fresnel: a lighting instrument that uses a stepped lens to diffuse the light; used mostly for washes as it does not have much versatility.

Gel: a square of color medium, which is placed in front of the lens of a lighting instrument, that colors the light that passes through it. You cannot use it in your hair.

Gobo: a metal sheet that has an image cut out of it. It is placed behind the lens of a lighting instrument. The light passes through the cut-out area—the negative space—and projects the image on to the scenery. Examples would be the shape of leaves, trees, the moon, or a logo.

Ground row: actually has two theatrical definitions: it can be a piece of scenery, usually just a few feet off the ground, that runs the length of the stage, masking any lighting equipment placed on the stage floor. Or it can be said lighting equipment, placed on the stage floor to shine up on to a drop or a cyc.

Hand-off: refers to a stagehand waiting in the wings with a prop to hand to an actor, or taking a prop from an actor when he exits.

Hazer: a piece of equipment that releases minute particles of moisture into the area, creating a haze on stage that shows the beams of light from lighting instruments.

Header: a length of cloth, suspended on a batten, that masks lighting instruments and other equipment at the top of a stage. Also called a border or a valance.

In-one, In-two, etc.: an area that is defined as being the entrance created between a set of legs. In the case of "in-one" it is the space between the first set of downstage legs and the next setup of the first set; "in-two" is between the second and third set of legs.

Legs: tall lengths of material hung stage left and stage right that masks the wings from the view of the audience. Legs also define entrance areas such as "in-one" and "in-two." Also called a torm (or tormentor). To confuse the issue, lighting instruments placed on booms out in the house might also be referred to as tormentors.

Libretto: the script to a musical, also known as the "book."

Logo: a drawing, design, or photograph used to identify a show or product.

Masking: cloth or other scenery that hides things on stage you don't want the audience to see. *Example:* Legs mask the wings from the view of the audience.

PARS (parabolic aluminized reflectors): a type of lighting instrument used most often for stage washes, where the lens and reflector systems are built into the lamp, not into the instrument. Par lamps refer to the lamp itself.

Passeralle: a runway that extends off the apron of a stage and loops around the orchestra, a la vaudeville or burlesque runways.

Pipe: see *Batten*

Practicals: most often refers to actual working lighting units placed on a stage for realism, such as streetlamps, table lamps, sconces, and chandeliers. Can also refer to anything used on a stage that works, such as a victrola that actually plays old records.

Proscenium: the permanent structure that frames a stage, often made of plaster and often quite decorative. A false proscenium is temporary and usually reflects scenically the style of the show. There can also be inner and outer prosceniums— if your theater has both, the area between them is often referred to as a cove.

Pyro or pyrotechnics: the use of small explosions, smoke, and fire on stage.

Raked stage: a stage that is higher in the back and lower in the front. Often looks gorgeous and is usually hated by choreographers.

Sampler: a stand-alone device or a keyboard that can sample sounds fed into it via a microphone or electronically and can then play them back on demand at the touch of a button or a particular key on the keyboard.

Scenics: artists who paint scenery or the department for stage painting.

Scrim: a loosely woven fabric drop that, when lit from the front, becomes opaque, and when lit from behind, becomes transparent. They can be painted or left black, white, or blue.

Soft Goods: scenery made of fabric such as drops, scrims, and curtains.

Specials: a light dedicated to a single purpose, such as illuminating a piece of scenery or a single actor.

Spike or Spike Mark: can refer to making a mark on the floor of the stage using spike tape, to reference where scenery or actors should go to.

Stumble-through: running the full act of a play or musical from start to finish for the first time. The actors tend to stumble a lot.

Traveler track: a grooved length of steel that holds the wheels (carriers) to which a drop is tied, allowing the drop to be pulled on stage or bunched up off stage.

Traveler: drops or curtains that ride on a traveler track and can be opened across the stage or closed up into the wings.

Trim or trim height: the height that the batten containing the scenery or lighting instrument plays at during the performance. When a batten has been raised to its desired height it is said to be "at trim."

Two-fers: a connector that enables you to power two lighting instruments from one cable and one dimmer. Also, a "two for one" ticket sale.

Upstage: the area of the stage closest to the back wall, and the act of moving towards that area.

Valance: a wide strip of decorative fabric running across the top of the main curtain—also known as the main header.

Vamp: a short piece of music that can be repeated until the next cue, often used as the lead in to a song or as underscoring.

Wagon: a platform that has swivel casters mounted under it and that holds scenery.

Wash: a light or group of lights covering a broad area, possibly of a specific color.

Wings: the area left and right of the playing area. Also referred to as "wing space."